Echoes of the Nokota®

A Memoir of Frank Kuntz as Told to Julie Christen

Print ISBNs
Amazon print 9780228632351
Ingram Spark 9780228632368
Barnes & Noble 9780228632375
BWL Print 9780228632382

BWL Publishing Inc.

Books we love to write ...
Authors around the world.

http://bwlpublishing.ca

Copyright 2023 by Julie Christen
Editor J Pittman
Cover art Michelle Lee

All rights reserved. Without limiting the rights under copyright reserved above, no part of this publication may be reproduced, stored in or introduced into a retrieval system, or transmitted, in any form, or by any means (electronic, mechanical, photocopying, recording, or otherwise) without the prior written permission of both the copyright owner and the publisher of this book

Author's Note

This book is a memoir. It reflects the authors' present recollections of experiences. As time passes, memories are echoes of events. Some names and characteristics have been changed to protect privacy, some events have been compressed, and some dialogue has been recreated; however, the tone and emotions experienced remain true.

Nokota® is a trademark breed name developed by Frank and Leo Kuntz and the Nokota Conservancy in Linton, ND.

* * *

This is a success story. It may not seem like it at times, but I assure you, it is.

This is Frank Kuntz's story. It is about how he and his family came to save the native horse – the Nokota®. It is my way of putting together a comprehensive collection of his memories and the events that led him to become the unsung hero he is today.

I have done my best to share both his story and the horses' story in a way that helps people learn, understand, and empathize. What might look to one as a life of sacrifice and strife is, in truth, a story of love and faithfulness. It is about allowing passion to drive your choices in life.

Since I am, indeed, not Frank, I have taken some creative license (with Frank's blessing) to fill in some gaps and bring his story to life. I have written in such a way that will allow you to walk next to him as you discover the man and the horses I have so dearly admired for over twenty years. Please allow a little grace and creative latitude should you encounter some muddy gaps or misaligned details. Know that, whether it be for loss of memory over the decades, purposeful omission due to emotional pain, or ensuring certain individuals are not painted in a negative light, the story runs true to that which I have learned from Frank and the few trusted individuals he encouraged me to seek out.

And sometimes, we must accept the fact that every person's story deserves a resonating tone of mystery. We don't need to know it all. Where would the magic be in that?

It is also worth stating that this book was written from Frank's memories, Frank's perspective. The opinions and attitudes expressed here are his. This is the way he sees things. This is *his* side of the story. He has a right to that as we all do.

Everyone knows you don't accomplish great things alone. Many people have played a role in the preservation of the Nokota breed, and still do. Rightfully, they deserve their own story someday.

This is Frank's story.

He saw something special in the native horses doomed for extinction in the Theodore Roosevelt National Park. He has spent over 40 years loving them and trying to find a way to help them. And even though the quest for a permanent home for his herd still goes on, the fact is, the Nokota® horse is here to stay because of Frank and his family. And maybe, just maybe, you and I can play a part of our own in helping Frank's promise come to fruition.

Being a man who is kind, humble, and generous to a fault, Frank's perspective is often hidden in the shadows. It is time for his story to be heard. He is, in my eyes, one of the greatest unsung heroes. So here, I will sing.

Dedication

To Frank and the ponies

Acknowledgments

This book would not have happened had it not been for the patience, advice, help, and encouragement I received from so many people. From quick texts, emails, and messages to long talks on the phone, everyone who shared their stories with me helped make this story special.

I thank Frank Kuntz for all the talks. The visits to Linton. A summer's worth of Friday phone calls with Frank. Random moments when the spirit moved. Thank you for entrusting me with your thoughts and memories.

Table of Contents

Prologue 9
Chapter 1 10
Chapter 2 16
Chapter 3 36
Chapter 4 49
Chapter 5 59
Chapter 6 64
Chapter 7 75
Chapter 8 79
Chapter 9 88
Chapter 10 96
Chapter 11 103
Chapter 12 114
Photo Gallery Index 132
Photo Gallery – Page 1 133
Photo Gallery – Page 2 134
Chapter 13 135
Chapter 14 140
Chapter 15 152
Chapter 16 156
Chapter 17 166
Chapter 18 171
Chapter 19 188

Chapter 20	206
Chapter 21	213
Chapter 22	219
Chapter 23	226
Chapter 24	230
Chapter 25	239
Afterward	258
Bibliography	259

Prologue

June 4th, 1949

Standing strong on a prairie plain inside the fences of the newly dedicated Theodore Roosevelt National Memorial Park, black as a starless night, a wild stallion cleaves the spring air with his clarion whistle.

A blustery wind swirls the stallion's mane up into a maelstrom of wildfire. His senses press out to the far reaches of the land. He is searching – always searching. His little band of mares and yearlings graze quietly below his overlook. They are safe, fed, and together. He makes sure of it.

The stud tosses his head and flares his nostrils. He seeks what he cannot fight to take for himself – others like him. His ancestors. His family. His people.

He cries out again. This time his call is threaded with lament – a cry for help.

He searches for one who would hear him. One who would fight for him. One who would make his family whole again.

April 4th, 1951

At the Kuntz family homestead in Saint Michael, North Dakota, a cry rings out from the upstairs bedroom in answer to that call. The fourth child, in the fourth month, on the fourth day, at 1:04 in the afternoon.

Frank Kuntz's journey begins.

Chapter 1
Winter

You're where you're at in life because of choices you made. If you want to blame the choices you made on somebody else, well, they may have influenced you this way or that, but bottom line – you made a choice. You made a decision. Deal with it.
~ Frank Kuntz

2023

The wind howls as Frank Kuntz braces himself against the biting cold. He douses the truck's lights to let the darkness cover them. All he can see out the windshield is a swarm of white anyway.

Outside, he hears Jennifer, his farm hand, cussing as she works at the latch on the gate. It's a stubborn one.

Frank squints out the windshield into the white-out conditions. It gets so dark, so early this time of year. He knows the horses are out there somewhere. Some of them are his. Some used to be Leo's. Some are now owned by the non-profit. In his heart, they are all part of his family, but he knows they all truly belong to the Lakota. They are descendants of Sitting Bull's war ponies, after all, and he was put here on this earth to care for them until he finds a way to get them back to their people. That is exactly what he intends to do.

He knows what he'll see once they come into view. It's been happening for weeks – ribs, hip bones, signs of hunger. Winter is hard in North Dakota.

He rubs his face with worry as he recalls his pleading voice echoing in his memory, "There's maybe forty or fifty acres of grass, most of it's brome, some crested wheat that's got no feed value after it's frozen. We gotta start supplementing."

He remembers hearing the reply from the landowner, "I got it. I got it." The same response he often got when it came to caring for the herd.

Frank is no stranger to battle. He has fought for these horses for over forty years. Frank has no intention of letting anything keep him from taking care of them, no matter what ownership is listed on any papers, or who signs his herd manager paychecks. Though his wife Shelly, his daughters, and many other family members stand by him unconditionally, Frank inwardly shoulders this responsibility to protect the herd on his own.

He made the horses a promise – all of them.

The aching screech of frozen hinges tells him the gate is open. He begins a slow crawl through the snow-covered path. The truck and dump trailer inch heavily forward with precious cargo – green gold. The hay he put up himself this summer with his 23-year-old tractor and broken-down machinery. He brings hay made from ditches, generous neighbors – whatever ground he could find, just as he's done most of the past forty years. That's pretty much what life boils down to for Frank and the ponies – hunting down the next crop of hay and scrounging up the next month's grazing fees.

His stomach knots up. Now he's gotten too far behind to catch up. He has to have his 185 horses off the property by the end of the month. Merry Christmas.

Once upon a time, Frank had been entrusted as caretaker of the herd. People counted on him and his love for these horses. They knew him well.

What are his options? It's not even a matter of David and Goliath. It appears he has no options. Even though he may question the feeding methods, the horses need this space. His own place's dry lots are already packed with a select few horses. Now, this snow compounds the situation. There is so much snow.

The herd needs this space.

He scowls at the sound of sunflower stalks crunching beneath the tires.

Jenn hops in the cab – winter swirling inside the cab with her – and quickly slams the truck door. "They're up there, Mr. Frank. Not far." She leans up on the dash, squinting into the darkness. Gruff and brutally honest, she says, "They got nothin' but straw. They eatin' nothin' but sunflow'r stalks and straw as far's I kin tell." Her thick Southern accent is strongest when she's mad. It's pretty strong most of the time.

Frank tries the headlights again to check where he is. This should probably be quick. He knows this place well – been renting these pastures for decades – but the snow blowing at a slant and up alongside them can be disorienting. As the truck rolls forward, it suddenly lurches to a stop. It's hung up on a sunflower stalk jammed right up the front end. He forces the accelerator and is able to break loose. He knows, somehow, that it's punctured something, probably the transmission cooler. More dollar signs swim in his mind. How is he going to find the money to pay for truck repairs?

And then he sees them slowly appear, silhouettes, ghosts of the past – the horses.

Their heads hang low – rumps turned to the wind – shaggy manes and forelocks protecting their faces. They are still. Soundlessly, they bear their fate. They stand bunched together, finding what comfort they can from the meager warmth and shelter of their bodies. They are cold, tired, and hungry.

Their ancestors on the prairies would have done the same, but there and then, they had been able to forage – even in the deadest of winters – for shrubs, bark on several kinds of trees, tall weeds, and tender grass roots buried beneath the snow. Though those winters were hard – many ribs showed on the best of them come spring – the herd's struggle made them stronger. Their bodies adapted to the gifts of the land. They survived.

Here, there is so little. Bent sunflower stalks poke out of the crusted snow. Although the horses can suffer a cut on the eye or face while trying to eat at these false promises of nourishment, at least their rock-hard hooves and heavily feathered fetlocks marginally protect them as they make their way through the snow-covered landscape. Always, they seek water, shelter, and food. If the moving waters of the little creek bed freeze up, they must risk their precious body heat and eat the snow. The gut must move, for the forever looming threat of colic could snatch them away onto their final journey at any time.

In the darkness of this stormy North Dakota night, comes a rumbling engine. The truck's soft, glowing headlights lumber closer and closer over mounds of snow. It does not come at them fast as though to force them to move, as so often the machines do. This one comes slowly, carefully, and cautiously. Then it rolls to a stop.

The dun mare – the lead mare – sensing no ill intent, turns her head and looks straight into the lights.

Jenn's throaty voice quavers in disbelief, "Oh my lord in heaven. Look at 'em, Mister Frank. Just look at 'em." Her voice bears an element of scarcely contained danger as she loses her words to take in the figures before them.

Frank says nothing. He only stares out the windshield as the frozen wiper blades sporadically attempt to clear his view. He doesn't have to see them. He knows. He always knows.

His ratty-gloved fingers curl around the steering wheel into white-knuckled fists. He clenches his jaw and works very hard to subdue the twitch in his eye.

How has it come to this? How in the almighty universe – after all these horses have been through – has it come to this? After all the fighting, the pleading, the negotiating, the compromising? After all the losses, the joys, the educating, the celebrating, and the advocating?

After all the dreaming. Never forget the dreaming.

This is all his horses have? This is the best he can do for them?

Frank sucks in a deep breath and runs a shaky hand over his face. In doing so, he wipes away the emotion then he gives a sharp nod. After all, this is not the first time he has felt this way, and it will not be the last.

"Yep. Okay," he manages to say over the wind and snow beating against the cab. "Let's get these ponies some hay."

Jenn needs no prodding. She is out of the truck in a flash and stomping through knee-high snow back to the truck bed. She effortlessly flings the small square bales they brought. Her bulky, worn coveralls don't hold her back one bit. The dump trailer releases its two round bales just right to be rolled out.

The dun mare is the first to move forward. Her keen sense of smell – even through the blowing snow – tells her these people have brought food. Though she is tempted to throw all caution aside and race to it, she stops short for but a second to regard the two-leggeds.

The man's eyes, deep inside a furry-rimmed hood, are filled with a powerful emotion that stirs within him. Because of this, she knows this man's intent. It is love.

Frank and the dun mare look into each other's eyes. She wades through the snow to wiggle her soft muzzle deep into a pile of hay. The rest follow her.

Frank exhales slowly. His life has not been perfect. He has made plenty of mistakes and made more than his fair share of bad choices. This isn't one of them. He made a promise to these horses long ago, and he intends to do whatever it takes to keep that promise.

For a moment, albeit brief, Frank and Jenn stand back and watch the horses come in to eat greedily. Perhaps as a gift from the spirits, the storm swirls up and holds its breath. All is quiet, even Frank's mind.

Only the sounds of contented chewing and deep sighs float in the cold air.

Wistful memories of the old family homestead flit across his mind – the rolling prairie carved with rocky, running streams. He shakes his head. That's gone now. Lost. And so is his brother Leo.

His childhood memories visit him more these days as his years inch on.

Chapter 2
Youth

If you're worth a shit, you'll remember the good memories better than you will the bad memories.
~ Frank Kuntz

1961

Pauline Kuntz yells, "You be sure to get your arsch home by *tree* on Saturday!" Her slight German accent gives her words a severity young Frank has no intention to trifle with. Sure, sometimes he might take other people's timelines more like *suggestions*, but not his mother's.

"I will," he hollers back, though his words are snatched up in the prairie wind already scooting him along the dirt road. He doesn't worry whether or not she heard him. He has other things on his mind.

Lessons are done at the little country school, and this summer, he's finally old enough to go work at the neighbors. After all, he's a fifth grader now. It's time to earn himself some money.

Warm, summery gusts tug playfully at him. He catches his cap just before it's snatched away and shoves it into his trouser pocket. He takes in a deep breath of morning, hoists his bag up high on his shoulder, and picks up his pace. The wide-open stretches of farmland on one side of him and prairie on the other give him a sense of freedom today, more so than any other day. A soundtrack of meadowlarks, mourning doves and sandhill cranes play as he heads for the next farm on the horizon.

It's a modest place, like most of the homesteads around Linton. Its familiar outline welcomes Frank as always, and as he makes his way up the driveway, several of the little kids come running out to greet him.

They hang on him and swipe his hat from his pocket. The littlest in her airy seersucker dress wants him to carry her. Frank hoists her up into his arms.

He says, "You're getting too big to be carried, Ellie."

She whines, "No, I'm not," and buries her face in his shoulder.

He smiles to himself and says, "Nice dress."

She looks up and beams, "I know! Mama made it for me."

"She does fine work, Little Bug."

Ellie giggles at his nickname for her and stiffens her body to get down. She skips ahead with her sisters and the dogs.

Seven-year-old Davie, trotting alongside Frank, asks, "You wanna play cowboys and Indians today? I made a new bow outta a elm branch I found down by the spring!"

Frank puffs up a little with pride. "Not today." He pats the bag hanging off his shoulder. "I'm here to work."

Davie tries to hide his disappointment, but not very well.

Frank reassures him, "We'll have to try out that bow next weekend or maybe tonight even. I'll be staying the week, just like my brothers do when it's their turn."

Davie's eyes get big with surprise, "You're gonna work?"

Frank keeps his eyes on the farmhouse ahead and says, "Yep. I need to buy myself a saddle." He straightens a little more and sets his chin in an air of mature determination.

The younger boy stops trotting alongside Frank and tries to keep pace with him at a walk, thumbs hooked into his suspenders. His face gets serious, "Yep. I'm gonna do that someday too, ya know. I wanna take my horse to the shows like all you Kuntz kids do."

A little smile curls the corner of Frank's mouth, and he looks down at the boy without moving his head. "I know you will."

The two walk with purpose in thoughtful silence while the other children squirrel around them the rest of the way to the house.

* * *

Mrs. Gross, fighting the morning wind as she hangs laundry on the line, swipes a long strand of hair from her eyes and says, "Good morning, Frankie. You can leave your bag on the front stoop. Go on out to the machine shed."

"Thank you, ma'am," he says as he sets his bag down and carefully takes out a carton of eggs. "Mom said your pullets aren't laying too good yet, and we've got plenty and then some, so here you go." He sets the eggs on a little bench and gives little Davie a see-you-later wave.

"That's lovely, Frankie. Thank you much," she says. She shifts her focus to her son, "Davie," she says sternly while wrestling a large, square cloth diaper onto the line and trying to fish a clothespin out of the bag, "you go feed those chickens. They ain't gonna wait all day."

"Yes'm," says the young boy. He trots off, but he looks back at Frank with admiration as he sees him stride off to the machine shed.

The sound of mild cussing and metal banging carries over the wind from a simple three-sided shelter on the other side of the yard. Frank walks straight in. Mr. Gross is buried under a little tractor. Frank squints and peers in to see what he's working on.

He says, "Can I help, sir?"

Grunting and clanging are the only answers at first. Then, "Frank? God yes," his voice is somehow both irritated and glad at the same time. "Grab me the 9/16th wrench."

Frank sees a calloused hand reaching out the tractor's underside. He scans the messy workbench and grabs the correct wrench off the pile of other hand tools. Quick as a cat, he slaps it into the hand wiggling its fingers impatiently, and it disappears into the tractor's guts again.

"Now the monkey wrench," comes the straining voice. "Reach down in there and hold that nut, will ya, Frankie?"

Frank doesn't need to be told twice. He does this kind of thing with his dad and older brothers all the time. He also knows he has to act quickly and do as he's told immediately. He finds the big wrench and angles it in such a way as to just barely squeeze through an opening that gets it to the nut he needs to hold.

"Got it," he says.

He feels the pressure against his hand as the torque to loosen the bolt on the other side increases. For a moment, the two strain against each other, but Frank's grip holds fast. In a second, he feels the release. A grunt of victory rings through the tractor's workings as the bolt starts to unscrew.

Frank's summer employer scrambles out from under the tractor and eyes him. His greasy face is youthful but aged from hard work in the sun and the seriousness of farming in North Dakota. Frank is used to the severe expressions on grown-up faces. He's watched his own dad's face grow more and more crabby-looking over the last few years, but he doesn't take it personally. It's just what comes with the hard life on the farm.

Mr. Gross reaches for a rag and wipes his hands as he says, "You're gonna pick rocks today." He juts his chin and squints into the rising sun. "You go on out to the field there and line 'em up all along the trees." He waits for understanding.

Frank nods and says, "Yessir."

"Once I get this blasted thing going, we'll haul the stone boat out there and you can toss 'em on that."

Again, Frank nods and says, "Yessir."

"You have breakfast?"

"Yep, sir. Sure did." The bacon, eggs, and toast his mom made the family this morning still fill his belly.

The man nods. "All right then. Off you go. Listen for the lunch bell."

Frank lopes off for the tool shed and finds a sturdy shovel then heads out to the field. The North Dakota landscape stretches as far as his eye can see. Sometimes, Frank dreams of what the mountains in his books are like. Montana, South Dakota, the Black Hills – he tries to imagine what it's like to wander through a deep forest, surrounded by trees that reach up to the sky instead of endless openness. He wonders what it might be like to see the sun stream down to you in silver streaks through the branches rather than across the horizon.

Maybe someday he will explore the world and see what there is to see.

As his foot drives the spade into the dirt surrounding the first rock of the day, his mind snaps back to his present mission. The dirt is dry and hard, but he thinks about what he will earn through this hard work. He thinks about a saddle.

* * *

The sun stretches up into the sky and beats down on Frank's sweaty back. He tosses a bowling ball-sized rock to one of the piles he's made and shakes out his stinging hands. He looks at the bloody blister sores with a grimace and knows he'll have to find some gloves when he goes in for lunch.

As if on cue, the call for dinner sounds across the yard. And even though his muscles burn from the inside out, his legs zip him across the field with little effort.

He sits at the table with his hands in his lap, trying to mind his manners like his mom told him to. His legs barely touch the floor, but he refrains from swinging his legs like a little kid. The other kids have eaten already and are now playing in the backyard or down for naps. So it's just him and Mr. Gross. It's just the men.

Joe slathers a piece of bread with butter. "Help yourself, Frankie. You're gonna need it." He folds the bread and bites half of it off.

Frank says, "Thank you, sir," and reaches for his glass of lemonade with one hand and grabs his own slice of bread with the other. His breakfast is a long-gone memory.

The man spoons a mountain of potato salad next to a thick slab of roast on his plate, then motions for Frank to do the same. As he sees the youngster's palm full of raw, broken blisters, he merely sits back and chews. In a second, he slides his chair across the black and white linoleum floor and goes to rummage in a large, wicker basket sitting in the entryway. He clomps back to the table and flops a pair of work gloves on the chair next to Frank.

He sits back down to his meal and says, "You're gonna need those this afternoon for pulling weeds and suckers in the shelter belt. I still don't have the tractor running quite right."

Frank looks at his hands and squeezes them into fists. "Thank you, sir." He looks up in earnest, "I'll bring my own next time." He makes a mental note to swipe a good pair of gloves when he gets home next weekend.

A man's gotta have a good pair of work gloves if he's gonna do anything worthwhile, he thinks.

* * *

The afternoon sun streams down through the thin canopy of shelterbelt elm trees that line the road. Frank has ridden his pony down this country road countless times, racing his buddies and brothers and going for Sunday joy rides. Today, he sees this line of trees as more than just mile markers. His dad had explained to him how the government initiated this "Great Plains Shelterbelt Project" after the 1930s Dust Bowl. The United States Forest Service planted 220 million trees that stretched 18,600 miles from North Dakota to Texas by 1942. It changed everything for the farmers here. Now that they're grown, the shelterbelts cut down the soil erosion and help the soil maintain moisture better. These trees mean life can happen here. They have to take care of them.

Frank, young as he is, understands this. Even though the shelterbelt is riddled with stubborn suckers, encroaching weeds, and invasive Russian olive trees – and even though he stands there alone and is expected to make progress on a seemingly impossible task – he pulls on his borrowed gloves and says into the wind, "Challenge accepted!" and gets to it.

* * *

On a rocky slope in the Theodore Roosevelt National Park, two young, thick-necked stallions rest from their fight over the small band of mares and foals. Their bodies glisten with sweat and are riddled with bite marks and scars. The small, slight stallion, black as midnight, stomps a feathered leg and stands strong into the wind, his mane a sail on the prairie. The steely gray stallion flings his head, tousling half his heavy black forelock over an ear while the rest wildly hides his one blue eye. Ears twitch and skin prickles as they oversee their domain.

Then, coming from the far reaches of the valley, they hear a vibration, much like that of the ground when the herd is on the move, only this does not come from the ground. Their nostrils flare red as their keen eyes lock on a black dot advancing toward them.

It is in the air.

They see it. A humming, whirring, rattling bird with a circular blur above its head. It has no wings, yet it flies. It moves up, down, and side to side, much like a bumblebee. It is coming for them. Somehow, the stallions know this.

The metallic noise intensifies and presses down, straight at them. Its vibrations are overwhelming, making their skin itch. Their instincts scream from every fiber to rise up on their hind legs and fight, but deep down, they know they must get the herd out of there to safety.

As the machine gets closer and closer, a gale-force wind whips at their bodies and beats sand and rocks at their eyes. The midnight stud makes the first move, biting his counterpart's chest, commanding that they retreat. Their fight with each other will hold for another day.

Together, they wheel and run to the small band.

The mares and young ones are already alert and dancing nervously in place, ready for flight—the thrumming in the air bucks their senses. Muscles tense, but feet light, the band moves as one. A clarion whistle from the midnight stallion cleaves the racket of *chuff chuff chuff* that is gaining on them overhead. His whistle is all the flee-bitten mare needs to spur her to lead the others. They will follow her.

The midnight stud then flings his head and whips his tail at the steely gray, sending him to flank the band, to guide them down the once-peaceful valley, and press them around the base of a rubble rockslide, toward the cover and safety of trees. Midnight brings up the rear, his ears pressed back, always fighting the urge that rages inside him to turn and fight this opponent.

The metal contraption whirs in closer, up against the mountainside. *Thwup thwup thwup thwup.* Its massive bug eyes bear down menacingly. It is trying to block them from the trees and push the band back out into the open. It tips its whirring, slicing blades downward into a predator stance. The horses balk momentarily, eyes wild with fear. The babies scream in panic as they nearly get trampled in the chaos.

The gray stallion looks at the midnight stallion. The lead mare looks at the midnight stud too. He must decide now! He whips his head, signaling the herd to keep going. The trees are not that far if they turn and race for their lives the long way around and through the rocky pass. They do as they are told and don't look back.

The legs of their ancestors give them pounding strength. The heart of their fathers and mothers beats a rhythm that will far outlast this adversary. They will run for miles, for days if they have to. Their thick, strong bones will allow them to wind their way up into the foothills – to the craggy, uninhabitable terrain if they must. That is what their kind is bred to do. They survive.

The powerful midnight stallion finally releases the fight that has been boiling up inside him. He blows out a guttural snort, flinging snot and sweat at the blades as he wheels around to face the monster. White hate flashes in his eyes.

For a moment, time stands still. The dust in the air, the strands of his mane, all of it is suspended in one noiseless moment. Then, echoing from the far reaches of his mind – Or is it the far reaches of the prairie plains? – he hears a voice that is clear and confident. The voice is young and strong. It bears a level of determination only matched to that of his own.

The words are a cry and a promise. *Challenge accepted!* it says.

Then it is gone.

It was but a fleeting moment, but the stallion heard the words, and somehow, he knows the one who belongs to that voice will come. Someday, he will come. They will fight against their enemy together.

The world rushes at the stallion again, wind pummeling him as he rises on his haunches and strikes out with slashing hooves against this impossible foe. *Challenge accepted*, he says.

The bug-eyed machine hovers, as though contemplating its next move. The stallion continues to rear on his hindquarters. He relies on his tremendous strength to maintain balance, all the while slashing and slicing the windstorm with his forefeet.

At last, the machine drifts upward and turns away. The stallion continues to rear at it, just to make certain the thing knows he is not one bit exhausted and could continue the stand-off for days if he must. Once he is certain the beast has indeed retreated – for now – he crashes down, hooves crushing stone, and wastes no time catching up with his band.

When he finally catches sight of his band traveling steadily over the rocky foothills, the forest trees in plain view, he stops to watch from atop a craggy hillside. He knows this is not the last they will see of the flying machine, but an inkling of hope – no, much stronger than an inkling – tells him they will not be alone. The voice had said, *Challenge accepted*, and the stallion believes he will come to fight with him.

* * *

Later that night, after Frank has washed up and said his goodnights to the family, he lays on his little cot made up especially for him in the oversized play area. The muffled sounds of children whining that they're not tired or that they need a drink of water carry through the house. By the light of a small lamp on an end table near him, he pulls out one of the books he's brought along. He would never leave home without at least one of his books. Frank loves reading. He especially loves reading the books delivered to the school from the Bismarck library.

The cowboys and Indians on the cover of this one draw him in. He's checked this one out before. It's got racing horses, men in cowboy hats or feathers, and the stretch of familiar prairie land in the background. He opens it up. Worn pages and foxed corners make him feel at home. He sinks into his covers and shoves his pillow behind his neck.

The pictures on the page and the captions are the same as the last time he checked this book out, but tonight, they seem different. Maybe it's the strange place with the strange sounds. Every house has its own kind of creaks and groans, of course, just like his. He just isn't used to this house's noises yet. Or maybe things seem different tonight because of the day he had. A lot had been expected of him, and Frank had met every challenge head-on. His dad will be proud to hear about the hard work he did.

His body and mind are exhausted, but he never goes to bed without reading a little. This night is no different. Except, it *is* different.

Tonight, instead of diving straight into the historical paragraphs retelling how the white men conquered the natives in the name of settling the West, Frank can't help but look at the drawings of the horses. There are cave drawings, pencil drawings, and beautifully detailed fancy-framed paintings. One of these paintings in particular captivates him. The native horses in it do. The caption reads: *Sitting Bull and his Favorite Pony.* Something about them speaks to him, there in the dark, creaking, unfamiliar home. Sitting Bull, looking straight ahead, stands next to his horse. His hand rests lightly on the animal's shoulder. There is no lead rope dangling, no halter or saddle connecting the two. A mutual understanding between man and horse is obvious here.

Frank shuts everything out and looks deeply at the stout, blue-roan standing at the chief's side. War paint decorates the smallish – almost pony-sized – blue roan face, shoulders, and rump with white circles or blue handprints. He looks deeply at the war pony's eyes in the painting. The horse looks at Sitting Bull. The artist must have really been talented. He'd captured the personality in the eyes. One is hidden under a thick mop of frizzy hair. The uncovered eye, however, fascinates Frank tonight. It bears a look of curiosity, mischief, kindness, and courage all at the same time, and if he's not mistaken, Frank would be willing to bet a nickel these two make a pretty good team. It's so different from the Welsh and Shetland ponies his dad raises.

There is something unique in the war pony. Frank can't put his finger on it. In the dim lamplight, he gazes into the picture for many minutes trying to figure it out. This stocky, sort of shaggy, blue roan horse – the way he looks at the man next to him.

Then he sees it. His breath catches in his throat.

It is love.

Frank reaches up and turns out the light then snuggles back under the soft patchwork quilt. That night, as usual, he will dream about horses.

* * *

Just like he knew it would, that summer of working at the neighbors flew by like geese in the autumn. Frank stands there on the porch with enough money in his hand to buy himself a saddle. Next time they go into town, he's going to pick one out.

He hears the screen door squeak open and then slam. Someone nudges his shoulder roughly from behind.

"Whatchya got there, Frankie," says his older brother Leo, blue eyes twinkling mischievously. He reaches over Frank's shoulder swift as lightning and snatches the money right out of his hands.

"Give it back!" Frank hollers.

Leo straightens up and starts counting it out like a snooty banker. "Hmm. I see here you are a whole quarter shy of your big brother fee, this month."

Something in his eyes makes Frank wonder if he's just kidding around. Most of Leo's teasing makes him wonder that.

"Give it back," Frank says again, sharper this time, and he grabs his money back out of Leo's hand.

Leo scoffs and scruffs up Frank's hair. "Geez, kid. Relax, will ya." He leaps off the porch. His bare feet painlessly slap onto the gravel, and he trots off toward the horse barn. "Race ya!" he challenges.

Frank, never one to turn down a challenge, crams his money back into the Mason jar he'd had sitting on the railing, screws the lid tight, and tears off after his brother. His scrawny legs zip him right along, and he catches him before they reach the barn. Frank is fast.

"I call Chico!" Leo declares.

That is fine by Frank. He knows Leo thinks Chico is the fastest horse they have, and that may well be true, but he knows that Sundance is the whole package – speed, agility, and fire. He grabs a halter and beats Leo to the pasture.

Once there, the horses lift their heads in unison. Frank slows to a stop. Gets his sights on Sundance. He shoves his hands in his pockets and starts to whistle a lilting little tune. Sundance looks straight at him, but Frank looks down as if he doesn't care if he ever catches him. He's just out here in the pasture to look at the pretty flowers and take a stroll.

Sundance wonders if Frank has seen him yet. Doesn't he want to play? The golden pony with the flaxen mane turns away from his buddies and walks curiously toward Frank. Once he gets so close that Frank can rub his forehead, he lets Frank slip the halter on and takes the carrot chunk from his hand.

Together, they head out the gate. Frank uses a fence rung to boost himself onto Sundance's back. One of these days, he'll be tall enough to jump up onto his horse's back without any help at all.

Leo, Frank sees, is still stomping out into the pasture for Chico. The little Arab-pony cross is not having it. As soon as Leo gets close enough to reach out to touch him, Chico flings himself away and trots off, tail in the air, to the sounds of his cussing.

Frank watches, like he always does, as Leo struggles to catch his horse. He wishes he could tell Leo to rest his shoulders a little and not hunch toward Chico like he's his prey. He wants to tell him to look away now and then, not stare him down like a challenge. He knows he could say these things to his brother, but it would fall on deaf ears. In the end, none of his ideas would probably even work since Leo wouldn't truly believe him. His energy is just different than Frank's. It always has been. They're brothers, but that doesn't mean they're the same.

Ultimately, though, Leo wins. Somehow, he always manages to win. He swings a rope around Chico's neck, yanking him forward to get haltered. Frank watches jealously as Leo flings his springy body right *plop* onto the horse's high-withered back. He gives him a swift kick in the ribs with his bare heels, and they're off like a shot, running straight for the gate.

The thrill of the racecourses through Frank's veins, but he takes the time to shut the gate behind them. Somebody has to remember to do things like that, or they'll be spending their weekend asking the neighbors to help them round up their horses. Even though Leo and Chico have a huge head-start down the gravel road, Frank nudges Sundance and leans in close with a fistful of mane as they bound into the ditch and head cross-country.

By the time Leo and Chico reach the end of the neighbor's long driveway, Frank and Sundance are already pounding down the tree line. One of the neighbor boys whoops at them from their front porch and bounds out to catch his own pony.

The sun is high and the skies are clear. The prairie breeze is on their tail, and all is right with the world. By the time they round a corner that leads to the lane back to the Kuntz farm, Frank and Leo have picked up a whole mess of other farm kids and cousins on their horses, hooting and hollering all the way. It's really not a race at all. It's just a great way to spend an afternoon.

When the little mob gets to the barnyard, the real fun begins. Horse wrestling is a true test of who's the best rider and who's got the best horse.

Leo gives a wild yip and runs Chico straight into Sundance's side and then wheels away. Sundance, Frank knows, can take a hit. His squat frame doesn't even waver, and Frank sticks like glue to his back. In seconds, he's charging his brother. He steers Sundance to go at Chico from an angle – that way, if they do it just right, he won't get too off balance and risk an injury. But Leo will be forced forward, or better yet, over the side, where he'll either fall off or at the very least, have to put a foot down to launch back up again. Either way, he'll lose.

Sundance brushes hard against Leo's leg, and Leo yelps as his tawny body slides up Chico's neck and over the side. For a moment, Frank thinks he's done it! But as Chico trots off snorting and flinging his head, Frank sees his brother still clinging to his side. Somehow – and Frank does not know how he or anybody for that matter can physically make it happen – Leo manages to scrunch his legs up so that the tips of his bare toes dangle mere inches from the dirt. He wrenches one strong arm over Chico's neck. Then, in one swift, impossible motion, he hefts himself up and swings a leg over his horse's rump.

Frank hears Leo's victory cry as he watches him and the Arab pony do a lap around the yard, but as his big brother comes racing back, Frank can tell he is gunning for him. There it is – that look again. The one where he can't tell if Leo is playing, or if he's out to teach a lesson, or get payback and then some. Frank and Sundance stand their ground, dancing in place, ready to dodge before the impact.

Frank and Leo lock eyes. They both know how this is going to end. Leo will win. Leo always wins.

The other kids in the yard don't notice. This is all good fun. They're having their little battles with each other too. They wield pigweeds and whatever they can reach down and get their hands on without falling off and whack them at each other.

The laughing and hooting turns to muffled tumult in Frank's ears as his heart races. His brother is coming for him.

Then – *ding-a-ling-ding-a-ling-ling!* Pauline Kuntz rings the dinner bell. That glorious clanging ends it all. Dinner trumps the ruckus.

Frank's mom is a magician in the kitchen. How she manages to feed fourteen hungry mouths, plus whoever else stays or stops by, is a miracle in itself. They have so little, but somehow, she can feed an army on a shoestring budget and a few things from the garden and pens.

Some boys stick around. A few boys call their goodbyes. They might be back for the Sunday ride around the big loop later on, or maybe they'll come back to play cards.

Frank can't help but notice menacing side glances from his brother as they call, "See-ya-round" to their friends as they trot off.

Frank and Leo haven't come to blows as of yet. Their dad had taught all the Kuntz boys how to fight. Some people might've thought his dad was one scary man, but boy, did he know how to fight. He taught them how to put on the gloves and have it out. Solve your differences fists to fists. Frank wonders if today might be the day he and Leo duke it out, but it fades. Leo's hot temper always does.

Leo laughs and reaches over to muss up Frank's hair. "Ha! You almost got me there this time. That was a good move – comin' up at me from an angle." His eyes twinkle as he tips his cap up high on his head.

They trot to the paddock gate, pull the halters off, and watch their horses romp back to the others. For one fleeting moment, there they stand, in the afternoon warmth – just two brothers watching their horses eat grass. Summer bugs buzz. Grasses swish and sway. The little creek in the pasture burbles faintly.

Leo gives a little nod then swipes his nose. He tosses Chico's halter right at Frank's face and takes off running for the house.

"Last one in's a hog turd!" he calls.

Frank shakes his head and just chuckles at his unruly big brother. Then he trots to the barn to hang up the halters in the right spots.

* * *

August wind blows like a furnace across the dry lot, kicking up dust tornadoes and rolling tumbleweeds across the barnyard like a John Wayne western movie. The heat and humidity make Frank's shirt stick to his body. There's not been a drop of rain for three straight weeks. It makes everyone crabby.

His dad has been a bear to be around. The second hay crop won't be "worth a shit."

His brothers think he's not pulling his weight, even though he is.

Frank's mother suffers from the oppressive heat. She's more easily irritated than normal at the littlest things, as are his sisters, which doesn't make life any easier.

The animals struggle too. There's just no reprieve from the stifling temperatures. The pump runs overtime as troughs are constantly filled from hoses running everywhere. Shade or not, everything suffers. They lost three laying hens just last week. And the flies, oh the flies. They're merciless. It's an unending battle keeping the cattle and horses from going mad.

Inside the stillness of the horse barn, Frank tries to put all of it out of his mind. The howl of prairie wind plays in the background as he looks at the saddle. His new saddle. Well, his new *used* saddle, but his very own – paid for with his own, hard-earned money. He won't have to share or borrow or beg to use anyone else's now. *After all,* he thinks, *a man's gotta have his own saddle if he's gonna do a job right.*

Dust whirls by the half-open barn door. Inside, it is quiet – a shelter from the heat and reprieve from the incessant wind. Frank loves being in the barn.

A film of dust and grime covers his saddle, even though he's only had it for a few days and had covered it with a spare horse blanket. No worries. He'll take care of it.

Grasshoppers chitter in that creepy way they always do this time of year. Even though they like to launch right up Sundance's nostrils and drive him nuts, nothing will keep Frank from test-riding his new saddle today. If he waits until after evening chores, the minimal relief from the day's heat just before sunset will make it more bearable.

He blows off the dust and rubs it with his hands. He rubs away not only the grime of a merciless North Dakota summer but also the dirt and grit of the saddle's past life. The guys at the local feed store in town often go to auctions to pick up things like saddles and tack to sell at their store. Frank wonders briefly about its previous owner, where it's been, the things it's seen, the things it's done. Then he imagines how good it's going to look on Sundance, especially at the horse shows.

Leo's laughing voice echoes down the barn aisle, "Still can't believe you blew all that cash on a stupid saddle."

Frank stares at the saddle, takes a deep breath, and looks at the silhouette of his brother walking toward him. "Yep. Sure did," he says back then keeps rubbing the worn leather with his hands.

"Phfft," scoffs Leo.

When Leo gets up close enough to see it better beneath the light bulb Frank has sat it under, he sucks his teeth and rubs his chin thoughtfully. His young eyes squint as he scrutinizes the saddle. He smooths a hand over the seat and skirt, inspects the stirrups, snaps the

Latigo straps and saddle strings. Then he lifts it by the horn to look underneath.

Leo makes a sound that shows a hint of mildly impressed surprise, "Huh."

"What?" asks Frank. Leo knows a lot about saddles. They both do – from reading so much – even though they rarely bother to use them. Frank is curious about what his brother sees in this one. "Huh, what?"

Leo's eyebrows go up as he offers a small grin and says, "This is a nice saddle, Frank." There isn't even a hint of sarcasm in his tone. Leo sets it down on the rack. "A little Big Horn tree in there. Nice and light. But strong too." He bobs his head. "Yup. Oughta hold up real nice for you."

Frank knows exactly what kind of saddle he got. He already knows it's going to be a good one. He just grins and nods with pride then goes back to picking at the gunk built up around the silver conchos.

Brother Leo musses his younger brother's hair and shoves him playfully. "But I'm sure we'll find some way to wreck it up good."

Frank starts to shove him back when they're interrupted by a booming voice. "Oh no you won't," says their dad coming down the aisle. He plops a paper bag on the little table. "Here," Father Leo says, "you better take care of that saddle. Damn-near cost more than the horse it'll go on."

Frank takes the small, scrunched paper bag and digs inside. He pulls out a single bar of saddle soap, a wooden-handled horsehair brush, and a new, soft cloth. He looks up at his dad, true appreciation in his eyes. "Thanks, Dad," is all he says. That's enough.

Brother Leo stands by, nodding and sort of grinning. Frank thinks his big brother almost looks proud of him.

"Well," their father says, "on this farm, we take care of the things that are most important to us."

"I know it, Dad," Franks says softly.

His dad continues, "That's how your great-grandfather Leo Senior did things, and that's how we will continue to do things today. Are we clear?"

"Yessir." Frank fills a small bowl with water, dampens the brush, and works a gooey circle over the bar of saddle soap until a decent lather forms.

His dad gives a single nod and then turns to leave, motioning with a quick jerk of his head for Brother Leo to leave Frank to it for a while.

Frank is grateful for the time alone. In small sections, he smears the soap over every inch. First, across the seat, which is just a hair too big for him. It's a little darker in some areas than others, especially on the jockey seat part. It shows where some other cowboy has worn it smooth, maybe from wearing chaps.

Once the seat is covered in swirls and up over the cantle too, he moves on to the pommel. It's got a few scuff marks, probably from a rope wrapped around it.

He works the soap down the supple fenders, already twisted the perfect amount from someone else's feet in the stirrups for hours on end. Frank's feet will slide right in.

Finally, he goes over the skirt. With its lightly tooled basketweave pattern, it's not too fancy, but just enough to be special.

Once he's got the whole saddle covered, Frank takes the soft cloth and wipes it all clean. He gets into every crevice, down every seam, until the entire saddle looks clean and rich. With this heat, Frank figures it'll be dry enough to ride in no time. Then his dad's voice in his head reminds him it's not smart to cut corners. Frank is itching to take Sundance out for a ride this evening, but he thinks the better of it and decides to give it a full day to dry properly.

Then, he and his saddle will start making new stories together.

Chapter 3
Moving

We stood there as a family and reassured each other, "Whatever it takes, we're going to do it for the horses."
~ Christa Ruppert

February 19, 2023

Frank drives slowly – heavily – down the landowner's long driveway.

It's time.

Frank hadn't been able to pay off this last debt to the millionaire by Christmas, but the endless snow had kept his herd there until now. A few days ago, however, he and the landowner had it out. By the end of it, Frank was told to remove his horses from the property immediately.

He grimaces at the memory of the words they'd exchanged. The language flung. It was clear, he had no other option. They are not going to work out their differences – neither financial nor how to care for the horses.

Shelly glances over at Frank from the passenger seat and says what he already knows, "This is the best thing we can do at this moment, Frank." Sometimes, hearing the words can help you believe them.

He just squints out the windshield and nods.

In the back seat, his youngest daughter Christa stares out the window and snarls, "Makes my stomach sick."

Her husband Brock looks over at her, concerned. He puts a quieting hand on her leg, but he knows his wife has every right to feel however she wants to right now.

They were all feeling it, holding their breath. Anxiety, anger, sadness, worry – all the emotions mix in a brew of the unknown. Today Frank's family, as they always do, is banding together for the sake of the horses.

As though the fates of change are on their side, it is a beautiful day. The prairie winds are calm and carry warm whispers of spring. This long-awaited break in the weather will help them take their mares to Frank's small farm just up the road. The snow from the wicked winter is finally at bay. The wind has been blowing the last couple of days, enough to dry out the muddy dirt roads. There will be no problem moving the horses into and out of corrals, and the gravel driveways will support the heavy loads.

Frank checks the side mirror and sees his first-born daughter Dawn and her husband Corey, plus his second daughter Alicia and Shelly's daughter Sarah, in their other truck and trailer following close behind. He loves his girls so much. It makes him so proud that they are willing to drop everything to help with what could be an arduous task. They understand these horses are their family too.

Shelly takes a shaky breath and says to Christa and Brock in the back seat, "At least Justice is watching the boys at the house, thank God."

Christa continues to stare out the window, her eyes glazing over. Jenn's teen son Justice is a Godsend. Just like his mom. Always so willing to step up whenever he is needed. It's good to have people you can trust.

Christa's voice comes low, "There's no way I want my little boys around if the landowner shows up. They don't need to be a part of this."

Frank grips the steering wheel harder. Though he will not show it outwardly, his body is tense, wound tight like a spring. He's not one to pick a fight, but he'll do what's necessary to protect his family.

The cab is silent. The crunching tires rolling over the gravel driveway and the squeaks and rattles from the empty stock trailer echo in their ears as they crawl around the curve.

Then there they are, a hundred or so Nokota mares.

Shelly rests a hand on Frank's shoulder. Christa scoots up to see out the front. Brock rests a hand on her back.

All in a bunch, the horses' heads pop up to see them coming.

In an awed whisper, Christa says, "They know. They know we're coming for them."

Shelly leans forward too, one mittened hand on the dash. "They know we're here for them."

Frank nods as he holds back the pressure building behind his eyes. A basal, protective instinct – the same one that has led him through so many of his life's choices – swells within him as he pulls the truck and trailer into the loading position. He shuts off the engine, and says, "Let's bring our ponies home."

Dawn and Corey in the other rig pull up into the loading position too. They all get out and meet at the fence.

So many neighbors and friends from Linton have offered to help today. "How long will you be out there?" "Do you need anything?" "How can we help?" They had reached out in earnest.

Most have known for a long time that the landowner's property is not the right place for Frank's horses. Even though it's this open landscape that the herd can roam, it is not their home. When word got out that not even weeks ago someone drove right through the herd while Frank and Christa were feeding, and knocked a horse with their truck, well, that was the deal sealer. Many of the people in Linton applaud Frank for taking the horses home. Frank is so extremely thankful to have their support.

Even knowing he has so much backing, so much support from his friends and neighbors, he can't imagine having anyone but his family here for this job. This is their task. Their burden. They will do this together.

The sisters stand united, as they always will for their dad. Frank can feel their strength. He sees it in their beautiful, compassionate faces and their determined eyes. It is a palpable thing that makes his chest swell. He is so thankful for his family.

Right there, his resolve is bolstered, and he projects that feeling as he turns his head to look at his horses. It is a tenacious look that speaks courage and certainty to each one. It is a look that asks them to trust him.

He asks them to come with him.

Without a whistle, without a call, without any prompts or devices, the mares come running. They know him. They know it is time to go with him, away from this place that is not their home.

Frank's family positions themselves in strategic places to effortlessly sort and scoot the herd. The mares file into the right pens and corrals.

Some will be staying because a few had been purchased from Frank by the board of the nonprofit organization, the Nokota® Horse Conservancy, which he, Shelly, and Christa were on too, since they'd initiated it long ago. Hard as it is to accept, he cannot do anything about those horses. He can only hope for their welfare and safety.

As though guided by a higher power, his horses practically load themselves onto the trailers. They are ready to face what comes next, for they know, if Frank is there, they will be safe.

As the first trailer-full waits for departure, Frank and Christa step up near the fender to see inside. The mares' eyes are not frightened, just full of questions. Some will be leaving their family bands and social structures on this day. Some have been taken from their friends. His heart goes out to them. They all stand quietly, together, in the confines of the trailer.

He speaks to them. "We only have a short trip to make, girls. I know this may not be ideal, and where we're going isn't that great, but I promise, you are going to get the life you deserve."

That same speech will be heard in murmurs and whispers from various Kuntz voices to every trailer load that leaves the land that day.

* * *

All morning, back and forth, Frank and his family load, and trailer, load, and trailer horses. At Frank's place, Jennifer makes sure the horses all get settled in as the rigs come and go. Though things couldn't possibly go any smoother, time is not on their side.

Waiting for Brock or Dawn to come back, Frank glances at the sun reaching high in the sky. The sheer volume of their task is making him wonder if they'll get all the horses moved today.

Christa, he can tell, is thinking it too. She's trying not to let her nerves show while she fiddles with some bale twine. "Sun goes down early, Dad. How are we gonna get them all?"

He hates hearing the worry in her voice while she shows her tough girl face.

"I mean," she goes on, "what'll happen if we don't get them all today?"

Frank knows she's wondering if the landowner might do something horrible if any of their horses are still there tomorrow. Though he wants to reassure her it'll be okay, deep down, he wonders too.

He reaches for the phone in his pocket and says, "Oh, don't you worry." He attempts an encouraging smile and takes off a glove with his teeth. He scrolls through his contacts. "I got a few tricks up my sleeve."

He turns away and calls a familiar number. It rings.

"Yah, hello," says a kind, well-seasoned voice on the other end.

A slight wave of relief washes over Frank at the sound of his old friend's voice. The conversation only takes seconds, and the phone goes back into his pocket.

Frank walks to the corrals again where Christa looks at him, wondering what's up. He nods and smiles at her then points and watches Dawn drive in with an empty trailer ready for another load.

When the sun starts its descent, signaling the last leg of daylight, still several trailer loads of horses need to get moved. Corey and Sarah maintain a calm and patient air as they do the sorting dance again and again, but they know there is too much to do still.

Christa finally can't hold it back anymore. She tries to squelch the desperate pitch of her voice. "There is no way." She flings her arms at all the horses yet to be moved. Then her voice shifts to near hopelessness. "You guys, there's just no way we're gonna make it before dark."

Shelly says, "Let's not lose faith," with her strongest, most confident voice, "God's got a plan," but even she is wondering just exactly how they're going to make this happen.

Frank knows they are all losing faith. He looks expectantly down the driveway.

At that very moment, a low, rumbling sound comes from a truck and trailer lumbering around the bend. Frank has called for aid, and aid has arrived.

He smiles at his youngest daughter. Joy and relief flood through him as he goes to the newcomer and directs the rig into the loading position. Once in place, a tiny-framed man wearing a black cowboy hat and sporting a massive, shiny buckle gets down from his truck. He takes a few bow-legged steps toward Frank and offers a hearty handshake that may well have turned into a hug if time hadn't been so pressing.

Christa yelps, "Big Dog!" and runs to him with abandon. She wraps her arms around this angel sent from Heaven and holds on for just a moment.

Big Dog's crinkled, gentle eyes go wide at first, then they soften. He pats her and says, "I hear we've got to get some ponies moved. Time's a wastin'."

She steps back, nodding, and tries not to cry.

Frank nods and says, "Yep. Let's load you up."

Just before dark, at that magical twilight moment when the day reaches out its last fingers of light, all the horses – every last one of them – are settling in at Frank Kuntz's ranch.

Frank walks Big Dog to his truck. "Thank you, my friend. Couldn't have done it without you."

"You know you can call on me any time."

"I'll find a way to pay you back, I promise you that," Frank says.

Big Dog waves Frank's words off, looks him in the eye, man to man, and says, "You'll do no such thing." Before Frank can protest, he adds, "I do this for my friends. And I do it for the horses."

Franks feels a lump form in his throat. It's hard to find words for that.

"Besides," Big Dog says as he climbs up into his truck cab, "I expect you to bring some of them over to graze a bit this summer, okay?"

Frank shakes his head in disbelief at this man's generosity, then answers, "I will certainly appreciate it. But *that*, I'll be paying for. No two ways about it."

Big Dog chuckles and starts up the engine. "Yeah, well, we'll see." He taps his hat once at Frank, and he taps it again at the crowd standing by the corrals, and then he rolls his rig out.

Frank and his family watch him go.

Jennifer's mild cussing floats into their thoughts from the other side of the driveway where the studs snort and jumble. She tromps through the pen, calling each one by name, helping them settle down.

She puffs up at one who looks like he might just try to challenge her. "So help me, Coyote," she growls at the stud, "I'd just as soon skin you than let you get by!" She locks such a crazed eye with him, the long-legged blue roan spins and runs right back to the others in the corner and starts snaking them around. He has to be the boss of somebody.

Jennifer loves these horses and everything they stand for. These horses saved her from herself when Frank took her in years ago. She returns the favor every day.

That's what Frank does. He is a caretaker to a fault, always one to offer another chance to do right, to do better. It's just who he is.

She hollers to Frank, "They's settled, Mr. Frank!" She wags her hands around the pen. "It's all good and cozy as they gonna git."

Frank waves back. "Alright, Jen. Looks good. Thank you, thank you."

She sort of mumbles a to-do list to herself as she goes off toward the house, her messy bun flopping on top of her head all the way.

Frank goes to the center of the driveway, where he can see it all. Leaning on his sorting stick, he stands at an empty trailer. He surveys the scene – this huge herd in this tiny space. A sick feeling roils in his stomach. What is he going to do now?

He watches his family filter into the herd to be with them. They're all concerned and just need to take a moment to be with the horses. Soft murmurs from each person float in the air at this quiet time of evening.

Shelly goes to her horse Bella who is standing with her head high among a group of pony-crosses, watching over them. Frank sees his beautiful, bundled-up wife wrap her arms around the big bay mare with the white blaze face. He knows she's closing her eyes and taking a deep, settling, therapeutic breath. That mare has a way of making anyone who comes near her believe everything is going to be okay. It's why Shelly loves her so much. If Bella had been able to take a pregnancy to full term, he would have had her bred many times. Her disposition is that special. After one too many heartbreaks of losing her foals to whatever it was nature decided had to happen, and despite her amazingly gentle attempts at being a mother, her role now is the *therapist*.

A sad sort of chuckle escapes him as he thinks maybe he should go get a hug from Bella too.

Up in another sectioned-off pen, he watches Christa scratch a typically ornery hard-keeper dun mare. A needy yearling colt nudges up to her shoulder and fiddles his lip across her puffy coat. He is offering some love in exchange for scratches too. Christa's giggle, laced with sad worry, drifts over the barnyard. Frank's daughters all have a way with the horses. It's in their blood.

It has been a hard winter, and he can easily see the dun mare looks thin and ragged, but Frank knows she does this every year. She simply doesn't winter well. As soon as he can get some real food in her, she'll turn around just like she always does. Despite the ribs and hip bones, her spirit rings true in her eyes. He can see it even from across the yard. Frank's dun mare will be just fine.

Auto and Firefox, the saddle horses, watch the events from the safety of their pen up by Frank's little cabin that sits just behind the house. The little bay roan named Iggy stands with them too; someday, Iggy might make a good horse for Frank's grandsons. It's good to see Dawn and Alicia go to them and give them some love. Frank hears their sweet voices murmuring to them, "Things will be pretty different around here for some time now, boys," says Dawn as the geldings dip their heads for her to rub their foreheads.

Alicia's voice is soft and soothing as a song, "We're together. We keep each other safe."

Every part of the herd has someone standing with them, talking to them, sharing space with them. All comfort each other, horses, and humans alike.

Frank turns to count the remaining round bales stored up by the road, partially buried in snow—so many mouths to feed.

It is a sad, sad scene.

This is not how these proud descendants of war ponies are meant to live. It's not like Frank doesn't know this, but the alternative is not an option.

His vision and the vision of others who've invested in the Nokota horses have drifted apart. Their ideas just don't match up anymore, so much so that, despite all the work they have put into the betterment of the horses over the last many years, they cannot come to an agreement. Since the beginning, their mission has always been to educate, promote, and preserve. Somewhere along the lines, however, Frank feels that money – and the ever-present grip it holds on some people's hearts – became the focus.

He looks down at his beat-up coat and boots. He grits his teeth at the thought of his tractor not running right again. He looks at the run-down house he has Jennifer stay in. It needs endless repairs. Having been released from the herd manager position for a few months now, he hasn't a dime to spare. What a kick in the gut. Caring for the horses – his own 185 as well as another ninety-plus head – is all he's known for the last twenty years.

How had it come to this?

As far as he can tell, it started with him somehow missing notifications of half the non-profit's board meetings. He guessed that some of those meetings were mostly held to figure out how to get him and his family out of the picture. Even though he would have been able to pay his debts eventually, he figures they decided at some point that he was a liability. Deep down, he thinks they just wanted his horses.

There was all the talk about money – how much could be made off these horses. What to spend. What not to spend. He had waited for grants to be written to hopefully help pay for expenses, but Frank hadn't heard of any being submitted. Instead, the organization nickeled and dimed everything from fence clips to the crappy pair of work gloves he's wearing right now. He and Shelly had to trade their horses to buy hay. It felt so strange, especially since Frank considers every horse he's ever had as *family*. It pained him because, in his mind, you can't sell *family*.

Then someone claimed that Shelly had made a huge mistake in the books, but Frank knows his wife doesn't make those kinds of mistakes. In the end, it turns out it had actually been made by one of the accountants. It was like every little negative thing someone could make up got aimed at a Kuntz. Now he, Shelly, and even Christa have been voted off entirely. For the first time since its inception, there are no members of the Kuntz family on the board of directors for the Nokota® Horse Conservancy non-profit organization.

To Frank, the thought is mind-boggling. He knows he is stubborn and tough to deal with at times. He knows he doesn't agree with everyone about everything, but to be cut out completely? He never imagined the board would cut them out completely.

The final wound, however, was when he got an offer to sell his entire herd at a fraction of what he considered his horses to be worth. It'd be one thing if the money would have gone directly to the horses. That much money could buy ten to fifteen days' worth of hay for the entire herd – that's how Frank typically gauges prices, in bales of hay – but the offer had been contingent. He was told the money from that deal would have to go straight to the land rental debt he still owed. Something about that just didn't sit right with Frank. So, being the stubborn German man he is, he turned it down.

Of course, being cut out and left to start over is heartbreaking, but he has to believe that, like most break-ups, it will all work out for the best in the end. He *has* to believe it.

He flips his collar up against a wisp of evening breeze. Frank's gaze follows Shelly as she goes to the truck to get the thermos of hot coffee and some cups she'd brought for everyone. The night cold chills to the bone still.

Frank and his brother Leo saved these horses to ultimately find a sanctuary, propagate the way nature intended, and get these horses back to the native people, the Hunkpapa Lakota. The creator had given the Lakota the horse. The white man had taken it away. Frank wants so badly to play a role in reuniting the Nokota with their people.

He worries that, no matter how many experts get involved in a breeding program, precise and prescribed breeding of *this* mare to *that* stud to get *these* results, isn't right. It isn't nature's way. He doesn't care if people think he's uneducated or old-fashioned. Give these horses enough space to roam like they did during Sitting Bull's days, and they will naturally find a way to thrive.

Looking around, Frank knows his herd's lines are strong. He will do whatever it takes to find a permanent home where his horses can be what nature intends them to be. He will find a way to make it work, one way or another. It's time to improvise, like his father taught him.

His dad's voice echoes in his mind, "Just 'cause you don't have the proper tools, doesn't mean you can't do the job."

How many times had he heard that growing up? The Kuntz family made up for what they lacked in money with drive, passion, and creativity.

He takes a deep breath as he watches the mares. Even under these dire circumstances, his horses approach every situation with level heads. They have each other, and they find comfort in that.

True, this could be his chance to get out. Many of his brothers and sisters have tried to talk him into getting rid of the herd for a while. It's too much stress, too much work, and too much drama. It's too hard on an old man in his seventies who should be retiring comfortably with his Social Security and disability check. It's all too much for a man battling cancer and PTSD. He knows they would tell him to sell the herd, take the money, and run. He also knows how right they are.

He feels like he's in a war again – one he didn't volunteer to be a part of this time. *This* war manifests within himself.

A flash of thick jungle strikes through his mind as his memories wrench him back to Vietnam, where he learns firsthand the ugliness of war.

Chapter 4
War

The central lesson of our time is that the appetite of aggression is never satisfied. To withdraw from one battle means only to prepare for the next.
~ Lyndon B. Johnson – 1965

1971

The thick jungle on the border of Laos creeps in close, heavy with foliage and dampness. Nineteen-year-old Frank, with his engineering unit, hacks at the undergrowth on the hillside. Their clothes cling to their muscled bodies. This climate and altitude make everything harder. Never mind the terrain they're trying to build roads over.

A cigarette hangs off his lip as Frank swings his machete and rips vines out of the tangled mass before him. The Agent Orange herbicide that was spread over this stretch just a few days ago hasn't taken effect yet. It will though. At twenty times the manufacturer's concentration for killing plants, he'll be amazed if there's anything green left on the trees. The pungent, musty smell was one of the first things his senses had to acclimate to when he first got here.

He takes a swig of water from his canteen, scowls at the funny taste, and looks through a break in the trees down over a vast expanse of hazy lowlands. A U.S. Air Force C-123 Provider aircraft soars over a distant swath of farmland, spraying more Agent Orange. A reddish-brown-colored fog hangs low over everything. The humidity over here is one thing, but the smell? That's a whole other thing. He'll never forget his first impression of this country when he stepped off the plane in Saigon. The smell assaulted his senses like a rotting, wet blanket doused in manure and diesel fuel.

Briefly, he recalls wondering when he was a kid what it'd be like to be in the mountains, to be surrounded by trees. The thought makes him long for the open arms of his beloved North Dakota prairie.

He'd known his grades weren't good enough to go straight into college, so he'd volunteered to go to Vietnam instead of waiting for his lottery number to be pulled, which may or may not have provided certain benefits for him as a soldier. Truth be told, he was getting sick of his boss threatening to ship him over to Nam if he didn't do this or that. Frank beat him at his own game. Besides, his brother, father, uncle, and grandpa had been in the military.

His parents, however, hadn't been happy that he volunteered. Frank had only ever seen his dad cry two times. The first time was when they'd lost a bunch of cattle to a catastrophic North Dakota blizzard. They'd borrowed a hefty chunk of money from his mom's brother-in-law to buy those cattle. The second time was when Frank left for Vietnam. His father Leo knew where his son was going. He'd been in World War II. He knew what war was.

Regardless, Frank knew he'd go eventually. It's what the Kuntz men do.

Now, as he screws the canteen's cap back on and knocks mud off the bottom of his black lace-up boots, he can't help but think how he has it better than most of the grunts out there slugging through swamps and rice paddies, never knowing when or where the next ambush will be. Leo had.

Frank would very well have been one of them had he actually gotten to Fort Lewis in Washington on time to take his flight out to Vietnam. He'd been home on a thirty-day leave after boot camp. He'd gotten in a mess of trouble for showing up ten days late, and he got a hefty fine too. The First Cavalry, turns out, doesn't care if you want to spend time with your folks for their anniversary before going over to Cam Ranh Bay on the southeast coast of Vietnam and probably never coming back. Frank had fully planned on getting there, just not as quickly as they wanted.

So here he is, building roads with an engineering team instead.

He goes back to whacking his way through the thick jungle. With each swing and slash, he can't help but think how things aren't anything like he expected over here. Oh, he had an inkling when Leo had returned just three months in with a .51-caliber gunshot wound in his hip and a head full of trouble, but growing up in a small rural area just didn't prepare him for how cruel people can be to each other. People in his own unit even. People on "his side," buddies even. Nothing from growing up, even with eleven brothers and sisters, prepared him for the way people treat people over here.

More often than not, and it pains him to think of it, the Vietnamese aren't people in the eyes of the American soldiers. The hateful, derogatory name-calling he hears when they go into town is as flippant as how-do-ya-do. In Frank's mind, it doesn't make sense. Their purpose here is as hazy as the air over the rice paddies. The TVs and posters just keep telling him, "For God and country."

Building roads, however, at least makes sense to Frank. Here, he's accomplishing something. The main artery road he is helping build will create safer passages through the mountains. He sees his progress every day. Maybe it will bring something good in the end.

"Kuntz!" the unit leader yells, breaking him from the solitude of his thoughts. "Get your ass in the truck. We're heading back to base for supplies."

Frank follows orders. He grabs his M-16, his flak jacket, and his steel pot helmet and climbs into the truck with the rest of the crew. They begin the slow crawl back down the steep slope. It's rough and narrow, but the driver and men seem carefree. They continue to creep down toward the little village below. The truck lurches to and fro with every tree root and sawed-off stump. Frank listens to the jokes and laughter from the men.

Soon, the strong, pungent smell of burnt rubber and overheated metal fills the air. The truck starts to pick up speed. The driver cusses and pumps the brakes over and over, but nothing happens. Leaves and branches smack the sides. Butts slam up and down as the men get tossed into each other. No one's laughing now.

They're losing control.

The driver orders, "We gotta bail! Now!"

Frank leaps free of the truck with the others. The vehicle goes careening down the hillside straight toward a rice paddy. Heart pounding, Frank squints at the figures he sees the truck head straight toward – a water buffalo and what looks like a person. Then with a cringing sickness in his stomach, he watches the truck crash into both, and they lie still.

* * *

Days later, on another run to the town, Frank sits in the back of the truck again with his fellow soldiers. He feels sober and serious these days. It's difficult for him to get in on all the playful jeering, banter, and gossip. He listens.

One soldier says to another, "Man, can you believe they threw him in jail for that burnout? Like it was his fault."

Another chimes in, "I know. What a crock. It cost me $750 to get him out!"

A resounding chatter of disgust rifles through the group.

"Yep. They charged $500 bucks for the dead water buffalo."

A sinking feeling weighs in Frank's chest as he wonders, *What about the person?*

The first soldier asks, "And did I hear that was a lady it killed too?"

"Sure was. They fined him $250 for her! Can you believe it?" He sounded like he was far more concerned with the money than the woman. "Probably would've gotten off for less if she hadn't been pregnant." He shakes his head.

The others scoff and mutter but quickly move on to another topic.

Frank sits with his hands flexing in front of him. *How could a human life possibly be worth less than an animal?*

The men's voices muddle in his ears. The muscles in his face tighten as an unfamiliar pressure builds up behind his eyes. He looks around at the rubble, mess, and displaced people everywhere. This town had been hit the night before.

Suddenly, the acidity of the soldiers' laughter burns his thoughts.

One man taunts, "Ah ha ha ha! One less gook!"

What are they laughing at now?

Then he sees a woman sitting on the side of the road, oblivious to them going by. She is sobbing, holding pieces of something close to her body, cradling the parts. The guys keep laughing and pointing at her. They roll past, and Frank sees what she is holding.

Her dead baby.

Never in his nineteen years on this planet has Frank Kuntz ever been so baffled by the actions of his fellow man. What can he do? He's just a private. No one would listen to him if he spoke up. What would he say anyway? The truck keeps rolling along down the road. He looks through the slats of the sideboards and sees a poster stuck to a wall. It reads: "What if they gave a war, and nobody came?" The words linger in his mind. They tumble and turn over and over.

What is his purpose in this whole *Vietnam thing?*

Once they park, they have a little time to walk around before the supplies are ready. He strikes out on his own. He just doesn't feel like being around the guys. He needs some space. He can't make sense of the things he sees and hears.

He decides to seek out the base camp's preacher. Surely, he'll explain this war to him. The preacher will make it all make sense.

He talks with the preacher. It is a brief encounter and a relatively one-sided conversation.

Late that night, he mulls it over in his mind.

Frank: I don't understand what's going on here.

Preacher: It's for God and country, my son. God and country.

Frank: God and his country? You think God would approve of this?

Preacher: The Lord works in mysterious ways. Just remember your purpose here is for God and country.

Somehow, his talk with the preacher made everything make even less sense.

* * *

Throughout his time in Vietnam, Frank is promoted to a First Class Private and then again to a Specialist 4. He does what he is told. He follows orders. He does his one-year of duty as he promised to do when he volunteered – for God and country – but the countless injustices he witnesses make it all feel wrong. Deep down. He is incapable of understanding how one can just disregard other human life. When it comes down to it, regardless of what insulting names you use, these are people defending their homes. He wants to speak up. Take up for the innocent victims like the woman with her dead baby. He wants to be a hero for those who have no voice and can't fight for themselves.

Fleeting images of his cowboys and Indians books track through his mind. He thinks about why those stories fascinated him so much as a kid. It wasn't just because the cowboys rode fast horses and shot their shiny pistols. It was more than that. It was more because he admired the Indians. How they rode into battle with hardly anything, and they bravely shot their arrows. They fought against a seemingly impossible foe. They fought for their land and their families. They fought for their way of life. They didn't speak the language. They had no voice. They had no one to speak for them. So they fought to survive.

Here, in Vietnam, he knows this fight is too big.

The nastiness of war seats itself inside his core.

When a quick snort or smoke of heroin is offered – a promise to make him feel numb to it all – he accepts it. The addiction takes hold.

* * *

The midnight stallion, many seasons older now, watches over his small band grazing in their peaceful valley. The leaves have turned brown and flown from their branches, blanketing the earth. Soon the first snow will come and lay atop it.

His nostrils flair. The air is crisp. His ears twitch this way and that. The deer are running to and from each other in nature's game.

A couple of yearling colts spar on a hillside not far from the rest. They're still getting their legs under them. Testosterone courses through their growing bodies. Soon, their chests will fill out, their jaws will round, and their necks will thicken. Their muscles will carve like stone under glossy coats. *Bite, bite, kick* is the game they play to sharpen their skills.

The younger gray stud that used to challenge Midnight has moved on to roam some other stretch of wilderness with a bachelor band. Midnight's strength and unwavering leadership maintain his position. Battle scars mar much of his body. The flesh wounds he suffered from countless hoof kicks and raking teeth bites healed quickly as is the nature of his kind. Then the hair grows back in a slightly different manner, dark or raised – tattoos to commemorate each battle. These are badges of honor declaring him the true leader.

It is a quiet day. Something sad sits deep inside his heart, lodged far beneath the comfort of his thickening, fluffy coat. These hills and bluffs, this prairie, it is all too quiet.

Where are the others? The other bands have seemed so silent for some time now. Have they traveled far beyond his little hidden valley? His soul searches for them in the far reaches of his territory and beyond.

Deep down, he knows.

He has heard the machine-bird many times over the years since his first encounter with it. Always, he has managed to move his little band to safety, out of its predatory attacks. Midnight somehow knows the stallions of the other bands have not been so wily as he. He somehow knows the machine-bird has taken many of them.

Others have come for him too, though. During the most recent spring, he and his band had been given chase by two-leggeds riding astride horses of a different kind. The sound of thunderclaps rang through the air, but there were no clouds in the sky. An unnatural metallic tang drifted to his nostrils after each boom.

The ground had been icy still in some places and muddy in others, as it naturally does each spring. This made it difficult to move his herd as efficiently as he needed. The old and the weaker ones struggled to keep up the pace he demanded. They would stumble and sometimes fall as the band turned sharply, veering away from their assailants. The two-leggeds' horses' hooves clanged as they struck the icy ground, hard and fast, but did not fall or even slip. Something on their feet gave them traction.

Midnight remembers the circle ropes twirling incessantly in the air. The whoops and whistles littering his valley's peace. His white mare had slipped, stumbling, and falling behind. He remembers whirling around, the herd pushing onward, as he went to fight for her, but she had already regained balance and matched his strides as they caught up with the rest.

The pursuers were many. Their horses glistened with sweat, and white foam slid down their sides. He could hear their labored breathing. They were weakening. How could they not be? They were definitely not like his kind, who could keep that winding, weaving, blistering pace he'd set all day long and then some.

Midnight's neck quivers as he recalls the scene.

He had stood strong and pawed the ground. He had flung his head in challenge and reared up, striking at the air. He remembers vividly how one of the two-leggeds had stared him in the eye, long and hard, then raised a long, shining stick.

CRACK!

Just the memory of the shocking, searing pain makes the muscles under a raised strip on his shoulder flinch.

An invisible foe had struck him and sliced across his shoulder. He remembers screaming in pain, then feeling the warm blood trickle down his leg. He knew he was no match for this weapon.

He remembers having snorted his hatred one last time before he wheeled in retreat.

He sighs – a deep exhale – then checks over his band. Their tousled manes twist in the autumn breeze to the quiet sounds of munching grass and the lingering whistles and warbles of meadowlarks.

Suddenly, blurry visions of a different kind of two-legged ripple through the depths of his mind. These two-leggeds have dark faces and trusting eyes. Their hands reach out to him – to all his kind. Their voices are faint, but he can tell they are calling to him. For reasons he cannot rationalize, his heart desires to go to them. His eyes scan his territory, but there is no one there. The faces are from the stallion's past, his distant relatives. They are the two-leggeds that once upon a time called his kind family.

Where are they?

He closes his eyes and searches the far reaches of his mind for another voice he once heard long ago, one that had said *Challenge accepted!* The voice that said he would come for them. That voice is quiet. All is quiet.

For now.

Chapter 5
Frank's Warrior

Be sure you put your feet in the right place, then stand firm.
~ Abraham Lincoln

Christa
May, 2023

It's been three months since Frank and his family brought the herd home. Somehow, God knows how, but somehow these amazing animals have found a sense of home – a temporary home, mind you – for the time being. They have found comfort in their closeness, in knowing they are with their family, and in believing in the people who care for them every day.

But today, a cacophony of piercing screams and gut-wrenching moans mixed with clanging and banging corral panels and pounding hooves riddles the air with sorrow and fear. Today, the infernal pain of loss rips through the herd once again.

"I can't do it!" cries the woman who's come to take some of them. She seems frantic and desperate which does not help her situation one bit.

Christa can tell the woman is on the verge of tears, and part of her thinks, *Good. Serves her right!* She feels her own tears welling behind her eyes, but a much, much bigger part of her tells her differently.

The Conservancy has sent a representative to collect their horses. It's true. The horses they want are indeed theirs, bought from either Frank's or Leo's herd at some point. The horses leaving today are mares who couldn't hold their own in the herd at the landowner's place. They are older mares losing weight who need extra feed, care, and attention. Also leaving today are the weanlings and one-year-olds that don't belong in the herd, plus stud colts that aren't ready to claim their place in the herd order. Frank has been caring for them for months on end, regardless of the financial burden it adds to his plate. He and his family do it because it's the right thing to do. All horses in Frank's care eat before he eats every day. If he's given ten bucks to spend on himself, $9.90 goes to the horses first, all of them. He takes care of the horses because he promised them he would.

Having been here for many months, the Conservancy's horses have made strong connections and real friendships with the others. Some have bonded to a point of co-dependence. Watching them being ripped away from what they know and who they love is heartbreaking to witness.

Watching this woman getting frazzled is tough too. She is hesitant in every move. She backs down at the slightest lunge, crumpling inwardly, and the horses know it.

Christa knows it would go much easier if she got down and helped. That, however, she cannot yet bring herself to do. She is here for her dad. She always is and always will be.

Even with the way some of the board members have been treating Frank – the cutting lies splattered all over social media – Christa can't find it in her to cut this woman down in retaliation. That's not how she was raised. All she can think to do is lift her up because that's what people should do.

After the woman nearly gets trampled by a couple of yearlings, Christa gathers herself and takes a calming breath. She hollers, "Rhonda, you got this. You need to find your courage and tell those horses where you need them to go." She barely gets the last words out before they catch on the lump in her throat.

Rhonda visibly releases her anxiety and gives herself a moment to get her wits about her. She seems open to coaching. Then, something switches in her stature. She stands upright with the borrowed confidence supporting her. She uses her sorting stick to help make herself big and stands her ground enough to get a yearling into the pen that leads to the stock trailer waiting for them.

Even though Christa is glad the process goes smoother after that, letting the horses go is emotionally draining. Hearing the other horses in the corral calling out for them, running up and down the fence line, wondering where their brothers and sister are going, well, it is another sad, sad day.

Hooves bang against the metal walls. Bodies shove and bump against each other. Then they are still.

When the trailer is loaded and the truck is running, Rhonda goes to Christa. She sucks in a breath and manages to say, "I'm ... I'm so sorry. The way the horses are neighing for each other. It's breaking my heart."

She seems to be hoping to have some kind of mutual, emotional moment with Christa, but Christa, try as she might, can't internally find any sympathy.

Christa assumes most people think what Frank wants for the horses is unattainable and unrealistic. *They've saved the breed. Isn't that enough?* That's probably how people on the outside think. It isn't enough. It has never been enough. It won't ever be enough for Frank until he finds these beautiful souls, these creatures of living history, a permanent home. Letting them go for a pittance, then watching the integrity of their bloodlines be compromised by human selection, is not an option.

Christa supports him one hundred and ten percent.

"You chose this," Christa says. "You all chose to separate these horses from their bands. You chose to separate their families."

The woman does not respond.

Suddenly, Christa feels her restraint give way. "And by the way, *someone's* been driving by creeper-style taking pictures of this place!" She flings her arms at a corner full of mud and manure. "And then they have the nerve to smear those pictures all over social media, trying to make us look like villains."

"I don't ..."

Christa's reins are loosening. "Do you think we don't know how awful it is to have this many horses packed in here? Do you think we don't hate that we have to put these horses in this situation? And don't even get me started on whoever called the cops on us. Ha! That was a real treat. But even the sheriff knows these horses are in a better place."

Mouth agape, the woman doesn't hold back her tears.

"Oh," Christa keeps going, "and you can spread the word that, no, it is not illegal to have this many horses here. In the state of North Dakota, they are considered livestock, and believe me, they are loved and cared for far better than any livestock ever would be."

For a second, Christa thinks she should probably stop. After all, she knows this woman does, in her way, love the horses. Her heart understands that, but what's happening is inexcusable in her mind. Her dad has been speaking up for the horses since the 70s. He has never backed down in his quest to save this breed and create a real, permanent future for them. It's a good thing he isn't here right now. He has enough on his mind, he doesn't need to deal with this sort of thing. She will always back him up. She will always speak up for him. So she goes on.

"And don't even get me started on how some of the board has been calling up people who have gotten horses from us – our *friends* – and told them their sale isn't legal, and that their horses are going to be confiscated by the bank. Every single horse we have sold has gone with a clean bill of health and legal brand transfer. It's *laughable* that you guys actually think the little bank we're using here is even considering heading out across the country to collect horses. They know my dad. They know that using the herd for collateral on loans is what farmers have to do sometimes. Not that it's any of your business, but I'm just saying. So go ahead and cry. I can't console you."

Rhonda has no faculties left for combat. Her face is beat red, her hair disheveled. Her body sways with exhaustion and emotion. She should know there is nothing she can say or do at this moment to assuage the animosity. Maybe she knows what Christa says is the truth, but maybe not. This woman has chosen which side she is on, and that will not change.

So Rhonda goes, and the horses go with her.

The only thing Christa's heart feels is, *Those poor horses. What they have had to go through, time and time and again.*

A final, wailing whinny sears the air as the truck and trailer pull out onto the highway. Christa clenches her fist over her heart as she allows her tears to fall freely. *What they have to go through now ... because of humans.*

* * *

Days later, sitting in his little cabin, Frank lights another cigarette. He's smoked too much the last few months. He drank too much too. It's not a good way to cope with things, but it's one of his ways.

What am I going to do? The words keep swirling around in his mind like the amber liquid in his glass. *What am I going to do?*

Frank remembers another time in his life when he didn't know where his life was leading him. It was just after he'd returned from the war. He didn't know where his path was heading. He just let life roll on as one must do when purpose and direction are elusive as wisps of cigarette smoke curling into nothingness.

Chapter 6
Restlessness

Not all those who wander are lost.
~ J. R. R. Tolkien

The 70s

The streets of the Minneapolis suburb are a concrete maze. Frank navigates the school bus full of first-graders down a narrow, one-way street just fine, but he has no idea where he's going.

"Hey, Mister," says a red-haired boy sitting just behind the driver's seat, "do you know where you're going?" He kicks Frank's seat like he's been doing non-stop for the past twenty minutes.

Frank admires the blunt delivery. "Nope. Do you?" he asks. He grins sort of goofily and looks at the boy in his big rear-view mirror.

Across the aisle, a little girl in pigtails giggles. She's munching on Cheetos. Orange fingerprints speckle and smear the green vinyl seat as well as her Scooby-Doo shirt, her mouth, and a little bit of her dark hair. Frank knows he'll be cleaning that up – and who knows what else – at the end of this route, but he can't help but grin even more goofily for her just to make her laugh some more.

The little boy shoves his glasses up high on his nose and scoots to the edge of his seat to look out the windshield. He points and says, "You gotta turn left right up there."

"Left right?" Frank teases. "Is that a left turn then a right one? Or is it a right one then a left one?"

The boy just scrunches his nose and squints. Frank can tell he's wondering if he's safe with this guy driving his bus but turns left on the block the boy had indicated. The joke of it all – and maybe a little relief – slowly dawns across the boy's freckled little face. He flops back in his seat, laughing.

The little girl giggles even harder and spills the rest of her Cheetos on the floor. She quickly looks at him with big, dark eyes and says with heart-melting earnestness, "I'm sorry, Mister Bus Driver."

Frank chuckles. "It's okay," and he means it.

Working maintenance for the Spring Lake Bus Company isn't exactly the job he envisioned himself doing when he returned from the war – much less driving little kids around on occasion. He misses the prairie and horses and working in the sun, but finding his way back into the normal world he'd left just a year ago wasn't as seamless a transition as a guy might wish. Conversations about crops, machinery, and the weather, plus casual inquiries of "What'll you do now?" felt distant for Frank. Or was it more like suffocating? All the eyes were on him. His brothers and sisters watched him without acting like they were watching him. Thank goodness his parents understood that he would figure it out in his own time like Frank always does.

When this maintenance job presented itself, he'd been ready for a change. He needed some space.

Coming back from Vietnam had not been a hero's welcome just as it hadn't been for Leo. He knew it wouldn't be. He'd completed his one-year tour of duty and came home to his own country that didn't feel very much like the same country he'd left.

Frank had known better than to expect a parade and confetti, of course. He hadn't expected much recognition at all. He never does. Honestly, he'd hoped *no one* would notice him. He tried, at first, to hide the fact that he'd just returned from serving, but his short hair in this long-hair era kept giving him away.

The recognition he ended up getting was the kind no one ever wished for. Being called a "loser" and "baby killer" among a plethora of middle fingers and rotten fruit from protestors isn't the kind of reception anyone expects. Frank wishes he hadn't been a part of it, that he hadn't seen the things he saw, or did some of the things he did. He wasn't proud of any of it. He wasn't proud of the human he'd become, but he'd chosen to serve. He did it. That was that.

He did try going to school first. After all, if the VA was willing to pay for it, he figured he might as well give it his honest effort. The state college in Dickenson offered a decent political science program. He could see himself getting into politics. After bearing witness to the consequences of some of the decisions made on a governmental level throughout his time in Vietnam, it'd be one way to try to make a change in an impactful way.

After a year, however, Frank's restless spirit decided the world of academia might not be for him. Sitting in classes all day, listening to people talk and talk and talk, and the whole college scene didn't suit him, so he set out to do a little exploration.

He needed to find things to do. He needed to work with his hands. He needed to seek out ways to soften the memories of war in ways drugs couldn't.

Right now, carting a bus full of first graders around a city he doesn't know his way around fits the bill. Making them smile, his finds, makes him smile, so this is what he'll do for a while.

* * *

The midnight stallion gently pushes his band over rocky terrain toward a valley they have never been to. This season of growth and new life tells his instincts that it is time to seek new territory. The winter had been hard, as it always is, but he and his band had foraged enough in the undergrowth of the woodland to get through it. The aggressive little stream had run strong throughout most of the cold time, and when it did freeze over, their hairy feathering protected their feet and legs as they pawed through the ice enough to drink. Once again, they survived with the tools nature gave them.

Though he has been on this earth a long while now, and though his black coat is riddled with scars from battle, the blood in his veins still pumps hard and strong. His wisdom has enabled him to protect his band and rejuvenate his offspring's strength. Again, now, he knows he must find another's mares if he is to continue his line the way nature intends.

They have walked for days in search of another stallion's band for which he will rise up against and fight. He knows that one day the age in his bones and muscles will betray his skill in battle, but as of now, his experience and tenacity still serve him well.

He points his nose in each of the four directions. A carefree breeze brushes his mane and forelock back revealing the hard lines of his round, defined jaw, and the bulging muscles in his neck. His nostrils flare. His ears twitch at every little sound. His keen senses probe delicately for any indication of others nearby.

There are none.

He will keep pushing his band. He will not give up searching. What other option does he have? He must do what is right for his family. Maybe the next ridge, or perhaps beyond that far butte. His keen eyes seek into the distant landscape streaked with red and rust, like haunting skeletons of mountains jutting into the crisp, blue sky.

Where are the horses?

The band continues down around a sloping valley. The grass is already turning green; a pale green hue peaks up among the brown mat of last summer. An outcropping of trees lines a river flowing with a strong current. Its crystal-clear water glistens in the sunshine. The high walls on the sunset side could protect the area from the harsher elements. It would be a good place to settle for a time perhaps.

Then, he hears his lead mare whinnying far ahead around a bend. His muscles tense at the distress in her call, and he lopes past the rest of his band. They carry their heads higher. Their alertness is palpable. They have caught a strange scent. He smells it too now.

As he rounds the curve, the lead mare comes into view. He stops abruptly. She is standing with her head low, sniffing at a mound in the tall, dead grass. His nostrils flare as he scans the valley. It is littered with these same low mounds. A pungent odor lingers in the air.

He gives a warning snort and a quick whinny cry to the rest. They need to stay back for now while he assesses the situation. His instincts are blaring *danger*.

Upon approaching the site where his lead mare stands, he notes the confusion in her eyes before anything else. With her head slung low to the ground, she blows out hard at the strange, dry, stalky squares she stands over. Midnight stops up short and then proceeds with caution. Deep down, he knows he should probably flee, but he continues to her side anyway.

Midnight snorts at the odd stuff and startles back. He scans the valley floor and sees more. More mounds of dry, stemmy squares. His heart starts to beat faster as his eyes dart around. He searches for an enemy but sees none. A short way down the meadow, he sees the unmistakable silhouette of a buffalo hunched over one of these mounds. It takes tentative bites and chews slowly.

Midnight dips his head to the ground and paces nervously. He paws at a smaller lump nearby and flinches at the odd smell that rises from its dust. It did not come from this dirt beneath his feet. It had been placed here. He snorts it out and goes to the others.

Midnight sounds his danger alert. They can't stay here. An evil foe has been here with evil intent, and his years of experience tell him they will come back for him and his band. Something inside him knows his enemy will not stop coming for them. This enemy will not quit until all the horses in the entire valley have been eliminated.

He gathers up his band, and once again, they run.

* * *

Building pools for Motel 6 with his brother-in-law isn't exactly Frank's dream job, but opportunity is opportunity. Many of his cousins and brothers get in on the gig too. Besides, it's a good, consistent, relatively basic job. All the pools are exactly the same, so the process of putting them in is too. Maybe it's not as simple as "Insert part A into slot B" but, once you've done enough of them, it's pretty darned close.

Being promoted to a construction supervisor has its benefits too. He is busy. He is moving. He is searching for his life. It feels good to work with his hands, put his know-how to work, and share it with others. He gets to travel all over the country too – the Midwest, the West Coast, and The South.

In Atlanta, Georgia, he, and the crew find a place more like a house than a hotel to stay for a while. Eating out every meal of every day, the food starts to taste the same. His sister Patty meets up with them and they find a place where she can actually cook some real meals for the guys. It's good to have a home base where they can sit on a porch and relax after a long day.

Patty, while cooking one of her chef-style breakfasts one morning, mentions to him, "So, we were hanging out on the patio, you know, and," she eyes him casually as she cracks eggs into a bowl and starts whisking, "there was a cute girl there. Guess she lives in the rooms above." Her eyebrows go up and she tilts her head at him.

Here, he meets Maria. She is beautiful.

Maria and her friend are indeed staying in the rooms above, and eventually, they run into each other. Frank and Maria get to talking every now and then. Originally from the Philippines, Maria's dark skin and almond eyes captivate him. She swoons at his shy, yet somehow confident, kindness. Kismet.

The thoughts of home that have been niggling Frank lately now dance in the foreground of his mind. He has considered going to school in Boseman, Montana, but home is where his heart belongs. That's where he wants to raise a family of his own, and since his dad needs help on the homestead, Frank decides it is time to go back to the land and the people he loves – North Dakota. It's time to go home.

He will work for the power company putting up power towers to earn a decent wage. He will travel some, but it will be a good job. He will help produce the cross-country horse races his family loves to compete in all over South Dakota and North Dakota. He's good at that sort of thing.

He and Maria will marry in the little country church in Saint Michael like the good German Catholic he is. They will move into a house his uncle is selling right across the street from that church. He'll fix it up, fill the barn with horses and other animals, and give it new life. Eventually, he'll grow tired of traveling and being away from his family, so he will stay home and farm.

Their first daughter will be born on Christmas Day in 1974, and they will name her Dawn – as beautiful as the new day she is named for. Just two years later, in the middle of March, they will be blessed with Alecia – she fills their home with beauty, laughter, and the free spirit of springtime.

Life will flow on like the Missouri River.

* * *

Stopping for rest in a wide-open stretch of prairie, the midnight stallion's lungs heave in and out. He likes this spot. He can see a long way here. Yet, instinct tells him he should take his little mob closer to cover. If the iron, bug-eyed birds were to find them now, they would have so far to run to dodge its attempts to trap them. He is not sure the young and older ones could keep up the pace that the distance between here and the line of cottonwood trees and rocky hills would require. He decides they will stop for a short while, and then he will have his lead mare keep them moving toward the little winding river and a distant outcrop of rocks and trees.

The young studs romp under the watchful eye of the flea-bitten lead mare. She munches on a mouthful of prairie grass and peers through the gnarled dreads of wind knots in her forelock. She doesn't want them to unknowingly wander too far as they play.

One young stud is much larger than the other, his steely blue coat blends into the approaching storm clouds on the western horizon. He rears up in play against his smaller friend – a red roan yearling the color of the hills and sandstone sculptures in the distance. The gray one wrenches his neck to nip at the red's shoulder. The red deftly avoids his opponent's razor-sharp teeth and wheels his back end around to let fly a kick that says he might be smaller, but he's agile and quick. The larger blue stops and stands stone-still for a moment. He lets the prairie wind blow his mane back. He is preparing to leave Midnight's band soon. He has learned so much from the alpha stallion. It's time for him to find a bachelor band and someday acquire mares of his own.

A white-faced black filly foal lifts her head and stretches her neck so she can just barely see the two studs play fight. Flighty sparrows cling to the tippy tops of purple coneflowers and sway back and forth in the breeze. Sedge wrens flit in and out of a patch of wild blue flax. Then, like a cobra in the tall grass, the filly's head sways in rhythm with the wind, and she lets the weight of her head flop herself back down. She dozes lazily and carefree beneath the bay mare with white socks. Her mother lovingly murmurs a prairie lullaby to her baby.

Midnight lets the prairie winds brush through his thick mane and tail and takes in a long, rejuvenating breath. Granting himself a small luxury, he softens his eyes for a nap in the sunshine. The earthy scent of sage permeates his senses.

The dreamy balm of sleep seeps into him, and his mind recollects. He has seen so many strange things in his life. He has encountered frightening two-leggeds of malintent. He has endured the absence of many of his brothers and sisters for mysterious, fearful reasons. Will he ever find a home where he knows his family can be safe? His ancestral instincts tell him he will need help finding such a sanctuary. This is a quest he cannot complete on his own. His thoughts become busy again with worry. There must be a way.

A voice echoes over the prairie. It is speaking to him. Searching for him. His liquid black eyes scan the landscape for an intruder – a predator, a two-legged – but there is nothing but sky and prairie grass. Perhaps it was the beginning of a dream, that's all.

Yes, it had come to him in his dreams long before too. The voice used words like that of a two-legged, but this voice had been filled with compassion – not confidence even, not assurance – just a promise of good things wished upon not only his family but his kind. Even though the stud rarely catches sight of other bands anymore, Midnight knows they are still out there fighting for the safety of their herd, just like him.

Then the echoing voice carries on the breeze into the distant hills. A hush falls over the plain for a single moment.

Then a soul-sweeping cry echoes over the grassland. A golden eagle soars overhead. Midnight looks up, and the eagle tells the aging black stallion that he will watch over the herd for now. He flaps his wings once then soars in a wide circle over the little band of horses.

Midnight rests.

* * *

Squirt, squirt, squirt. The metal pail rings as each stream of milk hits it. Frank sits hunched on the little stool, calloused hands squeezing and pulling, squeezing and pulling on the doe-eyed milk cow. The rhythmic sound and motion take him to a good place. Dust floats along a pinprick of sunlight streaking down through a crack high up in the rafters. Mourning doves flutter into the hay mow, breaking cobwebs. Myloose, the calico, watches from the shadows as she stalks around for critters. The smells of hay and leather and last night's rain flow through him.

Then Frank hears hushed voices moving through the aisle and stalls. He looks around for Dawn and Alecia. Those two partners in crime are probably playing some spy game or planning a crazy trick on their old dad. He squints out the massive barn door and sees the girls playing in the mud out in the paddock. Blue romps around out there with them too. That dog's a good babysitter. Frank loves how his girls can entertain themselves, so carefree out here in the country while Maria works at the video store in town. Maybe Maria will find a little bit of joy in this life one day too.

The whispers reach his ears again.

It's probably the wind winding its way through the chinks in the barn's walls.

"Hello?" Frank calls, his voice carrying high into the loft and bouncing off the rounded roof.

The murmurs and shooshing continue.

He pats the cow's rump as he gets up and then goes to the door. Brow wrinkled, one hand on the door frame's chipped white paint, Frank can't make out the words, but they *feel* like they're calling for help.

Whisper, whisper, whisper.

They feel like words of confusion, sorrow, and loss. It sounds like someone is calling for family, calling for home. These whispers weigh on Frank.

Dawn and Alecia start toward their dad, giggling. They are carefully carrying something on a piece of cardboard. He grins and mildly shakes his head at the sounds in his mind to focus instead on the very real, crystal-clear, giggles of his little girls.

Rubbing his hands together, he says to them, "Ohhh boy, what do we have here?"

More giggling.

Dawn says, "You're gonna looove this one, Dad. Alecia put a secret ingredient in it just for you."

Alecia, tongue sticking out with concentration, steps carefully so as not to drop her end. "Yep. You're gonna eat the whoooole thing this time."

The two girls stand proudly in front of Frank and present the gift.

"Another mud pie?" he says with over-exaggerated enthusiasm. Frank leans forward, hands on his knees, and takes a big whiff all along the length of the oblong-shaped goo that looks dangerously like the pies in the cow pasture. "My, my. You two have outdone yourselves this time. You're gonna have to teach your new baby brother or sister how to make these too, ya know."

Dawn's eyes sparkle at the thought. "Oh, we will! I can't wait!"

He takes the plate of goo from them and scoots down on his haunches. "What's the secret ingredient?" he whispers.

Both girls grin from ear to ear. Dawn laces her fingers behind her back and sways side to side.

Alecia, all smiles, sidles up close and cups her mouth with her hand to whisper in his ear, "Love."

Chapter 7
Family

I've gone through some very dark periods in my life, and the only way I could change myself was to realize that there are people and animals way worse off than I am. And here I am sitting whining and crying about poor me – I've always had my family.
~ Frank Kuntz

2023
At their house in town...

"Who's up for a road trip?" says Frank.

"Me! Me! Me!" yelp Frank's grandsons Beckett and Frankie. They both scramble from the living room floor to the entryway to get their boots on.

Beckett asks, "Where we goin', Grampa? Are we gonna go feed the ponies?"

Frankie, trying to get his arms in his jacket, yips, "Yah! Goin' to feed the ponies!"

"Well," Frank says as he bends down to help Frankie zip up his coat, "we're going to the hardware store and the grocery store and the bookstore..."

Both boys visibly deflate, but they keep getting their outside clothes on.

"And then," the boys perk up again, "*then* I thought we would go shopping for socks and underwear."

Both boys wrinkle their faces like they'd just been served worms for dinner. Frank puts them out of their misery by saying, "Ooorrrr we could just go feed the ponies." He gives them a whaddya-think-of-that-idea face.

Beckett and Frankie explode in excitement, hugging his legs and jumping up and down.

"Oh, that's what you'd rather do? Fine then. Let's go feed the ponies." He looks to Christa standing in the kitchen holding a mug of coffee and leaning against the counter.

"I'll be right behind you," she says and raises her cup at him with a warm, grateful smile. "I'm going to give Maria a call just to check in."

Frank says, "That's fine. Take your time." Then he adds, to be polite, "Say hello to her for me."

"Will do."

This is the boys' all-time favorite thing to do with Grandpa. It's also the best medicine on Earth for Frank, getting to watch his grandsons enjoy being with him and the horses. The time they spend together is pure joy.

Frank remembers a dark evening last winter when he failed to hide his sadness for the horses and his family's situation. He had been sitting at the kitchen table, and truth be told, he didn't realize he had been doing such a crummy job of hiding his emotions from the boys. The family works hard to shelter them from all of the sad things lately, but Beckett obviously had been paying attention better than anyone knew. Coming from his bedroom, Frank's grandson came carrying a Ziplock bag full of dollars and coins. He held the bag out toward Frank as he presented the bag to his grandpa.

Frank asked, "What's this, little man?"

Beckett told him, "I want you to have all of these monies, Grampa. So you can give it to the horses and you don't have to feel so sad. It's like a thousand million dollars! And look, you can even have this gold one." He points to a large gold coin at the bottom.

The tears Frank shed that night were filled with the gambit of emotions – love, pride, thankfulness. He also felt frustration and even embarrassment. He never again wants his grandchildren to worry about him like that, so he makes certain that their time with him is full of joy, silliness, and fun.

At the same time, Frank still worries. Frank always worries. He worries these same horses that bring all joy to his grandkids right now will someday become a debilitating burden to the family. It's one thing to make a promise and hold to it all his live-long days, but it's another thing to think of what will happen when he's gone. Like Leo. Leo's death sort of split the family. His brothers and sisters seemed to either pick a side or pretty much disappear, not wanting to be a part of any of it, which is all fair. Frank can't expect everyone to share his passion and commitment to the ponies.

The horses are a burden *he* chose, not one he expects his family to inherit. That's not what he wants his legacy to be. With his cancer numbers getting angry again ... he simply needs to find that permanent home for his herd. It's the only way. He must find a place where he can rest easy knowing that the ponies will be taken care of properly, without political interference. Their future will endure as nature intended it to all along. He has to somehow remove the responsibility – the time, the energy, and the finances – from his family. Frank knows his daughters and several others in his family will likely always want to play a role in the horses' well-being, but he loathes the thought that the horses could drain their savings, keep them from their other life dreams, or worst of all, become something they resent. If that ever happens, all of it was for nothing.

He simply can't allow that to happen.

"Let's go, Grampa!" orders Frankie.

Christa puts down her mug. "Dad? You feeling okay?"

Frank blinks his mind out of the all-too-familiar worries, smiles, and says, "Right as rain."

She checks to see that the pills from the "Saturday" section from his pill container are gone. Then she looks at him again with careful assessment.

Frank says to the boys, "Are you two *finally* ready to go?"

"Yaaaaah!"

He opens the door and lets them fly out.

Shelly comes up next to Christa and says as she reaches for her own mug, "He'll be okay." Then she shuffles sleepily over to give Frank a good morning kiss and says, "We'll be out in a bit. You go get a head start, okay." She pats his chest and snugs up the collar on his barn coat.

He looks at her, eyes so filled with love it's almost palpable in the room. They give each other a little peck, and he heads out.

The entire twenty-minute ride to the farm, with the boys chattering and bouncing in the back seat all buckled in snuggly, he can't help feeling overwhelmed with how blessed he truly is to have the most beautiful family in the whole world.

It makes him think of his big, noisy family growing up. The Kuntz home was always a-humming with some kind of action or drama what with each of his brothers and sisters coming and going and becoming their own person in their own way. One thing they all had in common was horses. The Kuntz family knew horses. It was in their blood. They could ride with the best. And they did.

Chapter 8
The Great American Horse Races

A race like this is a test of a person and a horse working together.
~ Leo Kuntz

1983-86

The cross-country horses and riders crest the distant hillside as if from nowhere. A collective gasp rises from the crowd as their favorite competing teams scramble toward the last leg of the Bad River Suicide Ride in Fort Pierre, South Dakota.

The sun glints off the horses' coats, darkened with sweat. White foam flicks from their necks and hindquarters. The riders grapple at the reins as they athletically keep astride their mounts and navigate from one flag to the next over the rough terrain. Sounds of scraping hooves against shale rings across the course.

Frank squints as he hones in on his horse Charlie.

"Come on, Leo," he mutters anxiously from the top of the stands. He's glad he's not announcing this race today; it'd take his focus off his horse and brother.

He locks in on his brother Leo's red and white pinstriped shirt as it billows around his small jockey's frame stuck like glue to the leggy dark bay. "Bring him home now," he says to himself, and he's not sure which athlete he's talking to. Both the horse and the rider are his family.

Lots of his brothers and sisters ride in The Great American Horse Races (affectionately nicknamed Suicide Races) that they put on. It's a family thing most weekends. This type of racing is nothing like typical horse racing where they run around in a circle at blistering speeds. A race like this is a test of a person and a horse working together. Frank knows his horse. Frank knows his brother. They're a good team, and they're proving it right now. Frank knows that it only takes one misstep to end a career, or a life, but he believes in them both. He never would have allowed Leo to enter with Charlie if he didn't.

Lately, Leo rides as if he doesn't care whether he lives or dies. The bitter residue of war tints every aspect of his life these days. Frank sees the deep-set thought behind his brother's sun-sharpened blue eyes whenever they talk about anything. He sees it in the way he talks, walks, and rides. Frank also sees it in the way Leo disappears – sometimes for days or weeks without notice. Once Leo found the wild horses out at the Theodore Roosevelt National Park, he started spending a lot of time alone out there with the herd. He spends his days with them. Even though it can be worrisome for those left to pick up his responsibilities, it's a good place for his brother to go when he needs space.

Frank gets that, one hundred percent. He knows how the images of war can swoop into the foreground of your mind without warning like demons. He understands, firsthand, how hard it is to fight them and find your way back to "normal". Frank knows how – even when you think you've got them whipped and shoved down good and deep – they flicker like flames that lick up behind even your best thoughts on your best days.

Frank's daughters are his most valuable warriors against his demons. When he feels the dragging weight of horrific memories and hears echoes of frightened screaming children and crying women, Dawn's sweet voice and Alecia's dancing eyes help him hold it together a little longer than the last time. His heart swells to think he has another baby on the way this Christmas season,

He focuses on showing his girls how to be good people. He wants so badly to make sure they know how beautiful they are, inside and out. He knows they have to deal with kids at school making smart-aleck remarks about their dark skin and almond-shaped eyes. He thanks the Maker for their close, trusting relationship. He wants them to feel comfortable seeking him out as a listening ear. He will remind them, every hour of every day if need be, that they are an important part of this world.

If he does this – if he can do right by them and show them that they have all the tools they need to make their way through this tough world with grace and empathy – then those demons certainly will have their hands full. Those licking flames of memory will subside. Though he knows they will never disappear entirely, he will live to fight another day.

What does Leo have?

Frank focuses intently on his brother and Charlie out on the course. He sees them sliding down the final slope ahead of the others. Even from this distance, he can tell that Leo is clinging like a spider monkey to his horse. His moccasin feet are folded, close and tight, to the bay's glistening barrel. Frank feels pride for his brother and his talents. It's a little sad, in some ways, that Leo still hasn't found a special someone to share his life with and start a family like he has with Maria. How had Leo put it the last time one of their sisters or someone had brought it up? "I don't want to affect anyone else's life, especially in a bad way."

Whenever the topic of marriage got brought up around him, he'd find some clever way to avoid the conversation altogether. Leo believes that sometimes solitary is the best for everyone involved. That's how he stays – alone, for the most part. Besides, he's always said he'd have to be rich if he was going to get married, so he could "take care of the little woman and whatever." Frank knows too well, however, that the

Kuntz men are stubborn. They were born poor and they'll make sure they die that way.

Charlie racks his body jerkily down the hill. His hooves jackhammer against the ground. Frank knows the beating his horse's joints take from the concussive force of a thousand-plus pounds driving down, down, down at breakneck speed. He trains his sights on the ground they still have to cover. Boulders hunch like predators. Clusters of craggy rocks mixed with smooth, flat stones riddle their path like land mines. After that stretch, they're in the clear. A grassy, flat homestretch will bring them back to the stadium and the roar of the cheering crowd.

Frank's brow knits with the intensity of it all. *God, if anything happens to them ...*

Yes, this is a big race. The prize money is no joke. Images of rusty, broken equipment, run-down fences, and sagging buildings clog his mind. It had also taken a lot of time and resources (two commodities he seems to be in short supply of these days) to get them there – sponsors, entry fees, food, entertainment, whatever – but no prize, no glory, no dollar amount is worth losing either of them over.

Charlie's hind hoof catches on a sharp rock jutting up from the rubble. In a flash, the bay's hindquarters go down, but his momentum keeps them moving forward. Leo glances backward, which tosses him in one lurching movement onto Charlie's sweaty rump. In an impossible scramble, Leo lurches for the horse's mane, grabs fistfuls of hair with both hands, and – in a way only Leo Kuntz is capable of – pulls himself right again. It all happens in the space of seconds, and they are up crossing a short bit of flat rocks. Even from where he stands, he can hear the harsh scraping sounds. It sets Frank's teeth on edge. Charlie has to rely on sheer balance and speed to get across. He's got nothing to help his grip. Leo sits tight, stone still, trusting Charlie to navigate as he sees fit.

Charlie slips – once. His right front almost imperceptibly jaunts out awkwardly. Leo urges him on. The one-and-a-half-mile race is nearly theirs!

All the riders' yips and haws trickle on the prairie wind toward the crowd waiting at the finish line. Their cheers go up like a blast of fireworks against the cloudless sky, and Frank sees his horse's ears press forward. At this moment, Frank's chest fills with pride. It courses through his veins as though lending his own pulse of energy to channel into Charlie for his last, heroic push to victory and safety.

After having their picture taken with Charlie and accepting their prize, Frank and Leo walk the horse back to the stables together. Frank watches for any misstep or show of injury. He stops to feel Charlie's right front leg for any heat.

"Ya," says Leo running his fingers through his hair, "I figured you saw that slip." His voice suddenly takes on a defensive edge. "Don't go getting' all worked up about it now. I know how to ride."

Frank says, "I know you know how to ride." He cuts himself off there, though. Like when they were kids, he knows how Leo's temper can flare at the littlest thing, and it's just as easy to get caught up in an argument with him now that they're both grown men as it was when they were young. Only now, they didn't have to worry about the wrath of their dad and a clonk on the head to break them up. Besides, that's not what Frank's going for anyway. He simply wants to check his horse over.

Frank raises both his hands in a settle-down kind of gesture and goes back to feeling for heat in the rest of Charlie's legs.

Leo is quiet for a second then asks with a tiny hint of concern, "How's it feel?"

Frank hides his sigh of relief. "Just fine."

Leo pats Charlie's neck as they continue on. "Ya, I figured so. He's a good horse, this one."

Frank nods, but something inside him still worries. "You know, Leo, Charlie's pushin' 9 or 10 years old here. I mean, really, this should be his prime time, but jeez if I don't wonder."

Charlie is a running quarter with a mix of thoroughbred in him just like a lot of people are using in these races. He's a good, solid horse, but Frank and Leo are noticing lately that when they get to be around 8 or 9 when they should be in their prime, they seem to be starting to break down already.

A gaggle of kids go running past. Dawn and Alecia have long since abandoned their post where they are supposed to be selling programs and flyers for the races that day. Frank sees one of his sisters and a couple of the older kids have taken over while the girls and their cousins run around playing and laughing and generally staying out of the grown-ups' way as they'd been told.

Charlie thoroughly enjoys his rub-down and blows out a contented sigh as he slurps a little water from the bucket hanging in the corner of his corral. Frank and Leo lean on the rails and watch as he rolls on the ground and moans in delight. The thousand-pound animal grinds his muscles into the dirt. Then he pops up effortlessly and shimmy-shakes his entire body. A cloud of dust billows away from him and is wafted away in the breeze. He blows out an indulgent, snotty snort. Finally, he goes to nibble at the flake of hay he knows he's completely earned.

"I got an idea," says Leo.

Frank looks at him and turns around to lean his back against the corral fence. Leo sticks a long blade of grass in his mouth and turns around too. They hook their thumbs in their pockets and look out over the general buzz of activity throughout the grounds. Leo aims his gaze out across the wide-open, rolling landscape. Frank can tell by the look in his brother's eyes that whatever his idea is, it's something he's been thinking about for a while, something important to him.

"Oh?" Frank says. "What's that?"

Leo meets Frank's eyes quickly and earnestly, then blinks away and looks back to the horizon, "You know Bad Toe?" A small, mischievous smile curls up one side of his mouth.

"Of course, I know Bad Toe," says Frank, wondering where he was going with this.

Bad Toe was one of a couple of horses Leo got back in '79 from some ranchers in the Medora area. Leo had been hell-bent on nabbing himself one of those horses he spent so much time with at the park. Once, he even managed to catch a mare barehanded on horseback. He just got up alongside close enough to grab her by the mane, and that was that. Frank will never forget how that seemed to be a sort of life-changing moment for his brother, for the good this time.

A trail riding outfit had gathered several horses from one of the park's round-ups and was trying to sell some "feral ranch stock" as they put it, but Bad Toe proves those horses out there are so much more than feral ranch stock. He's sure-footed on broken ground, speedy on the flats, has deep lungs, and an even bigger heart. He's often Leo's go-to racehorse, and he's showing better brains and agility than most of the domestic racing horses around.

"What about Bad Toe?" Frank asks.

Frank has had his own ideas about the park horses too. Plus, Frank knows that look Leo's giving him. It's the very same grin he has known all their lives, the one that says Leo's got a bright idea and nothing's going to hold him back. Frank also knows that continuing whatever conversation they're about to have will more than likely lead to an endeavor that will require his involvement, one way or another.

He looks at his girls across the arena grounds. Alecia squeals with delight as Dawn tosses a ratty, looped rope over her head, and they go running around the stands. He thinks of all the things he wants them to have in life. He thinks about the FHA loan he's got on his home and rumors of interest rates rising to as high as 17% soon. He's strapped for time and money enough the way things are right now. He hardly has time to entertain some crazy scheme Leo's dreaming up.

Then he realizes he's probably over-thinking this. After all, Leo's probably just planning to take another road trip vacation with Bad Toe.

"I'm thinking," Leo repeats, "I want you to take a look at some horses with me. Out at the park."

Frank breathes out in a chuckle. *Definitely overthought that.* "Some horses, huh?"

His brother says, "Yup. Out at the park." His head bounces slightly like he's convincing himself of something.

Leo's gaze hasn't left distant hills. That look tells Frank something is up.

Frank sees the normal backdrop of sadness in his brother's eyes briefly replaced by a flicker of happiness. It's mingled with a spark of something like excitement, or maybe hope. Regardless, it's the truest expression he's seen from his brother in a while. Leo comes across as the happy-go-lucky one all the time. Adventure seeker extraordinaire. Frank knows better. This moment makes Frank feel like whatever he's about to get himself roped into will be worth it if just to see his brother genuinely happy.

After a long stretch of silence between them, Leo finally turns to look his younger brother in the eye. He says to Frank, "I've been watching those wild ones out there for a long time. They're different. Ya know what I mean? They been rounin' 'em up too. Park wants to get rid of 'em." He pauses. "I got an idea about them. I been doin' some research, ya know, and I think there's really somethin' about those ponies. They could make a big difference in our racehorse bloodlines. Their bones. Their brains." He takes a breath. "I just got a good feeling about 'em. We need to add 'em to our breeding program."

Frank takes a moment to digest the gravity in Leo's voice and this idea. He's seen the wild horses out in the Theodore Roosevelt National Park several times. The Kuntz family goes to Medora all the time. His folks take their ponies in and do the carriage rides around town for the tourists. He knows the place well, just maybe not as much as Leo these days. Leo spends an awful lot of time out there. Whatever he's thinking, Frank figures, it isn't just a whim.

Frank bounces his head and looks out over the landscape now. His own eyes are serious as is his voice. "Okay. Let's go take a look at some horses."

Leo gives him a quick glance that briefly resembles a *Thank you, brother*, and then it's whisked away as a crowd of family hoots and hollers to them.

Their younger sister Felicia hollers, "Hey Frank! Got any plans for setting up the dance? People are asking."

Frank hollers back with a slightly forced grin, "Yup. I'm on it."

Leo looks down and chuckles.

Frank lands a strong hand on Leo's shoulder and says with a head-shake laugh, "Work is never done."

"Nope. Sure ain't. You better git before she threatens to take over."

They give each other a knowing, slightly terrified look.

Frank starts off and then turns back to his brother. "We'll go see the horses."

Chapter 9
Purpose

The purpose of life is to find your mission and fulfill it.
~ Mother Teresa

1984-86 Continued...

Somewhere in the South Unit of the Theodore Roosevelt National Park, Frank and Leo stand on an outcrop of rocks on the edge of a prairie valley. The Little Missouri River meanders in the backdrop, and the distant horizon is etched with medieval-looking spires of sandstone that jut into the sky. Cottonwood trees line the edge of the ruff hillsides of ever-changing, sliding shale. Painted valleys create a breathtaking vista in one direction and sweeping grasslands course for miles in another.

It's enough to take a man's breath away. Frank drinks in the beauty and the solitude. This place was truly created to give man pause. It's no wonder Leo keeps coming back. It takes his mind to a place of peace. The deafening quiet, save the playful breeze sweeping over the terrain, soothes his aches and pains, inside and out.

"I don't see 'em just yet," says Leo as he scans the common spots he usually finds a band of wild horses.

Frank is quiet.

"Trust me, they'll be here somewhere." He sounds a little anxious, almost irritated. "We just gotta wait sometimes."

"Yeah." Frank takes a few steps to the edge of the outcrop of rocks while Leo backtracks on the trail they came in on.

Alone with the expanse of space, he lets the breeze brush past him, carrying his scent out into the grassland below. Maybe that's what's holding them back. They smell a stranger. His keen eyes sweep the landscape as his shoulders relax. The wind gusts from behind a little more, so he stoops down to one knee and picks a few long blades of grass to fiddle with.

The prairie breeze swoops and soars whimsically down the slope, skimming the tops of wildflowers, and racing the grasshoppers over the grass. As it curls around a bend at the base of a cottonwood-covered hill and filters through the trees, it reaches the little band of horses.

Midnight raises his head as the breeze carries a strange scent. It makes him shake his head and tousle his mane. He can tell it is a two-legged, but not the same two-legged that has been here many times before – the one he has seen watching his little band from afar, just sitting in one place while the sun travels across the sky. It is not the one who sometimes tries to walk among them and offer an outstretched hand. That two-legged has a distinct smell – no, not just smell – energy, a vibration of longing, of need. Midnight still has not deduced what his intent is exactly, but he carries no sharp things, or loud things, and clearly has no intent to do them harm as of yet.

This new scent carries something very different, almost familiar like an echo from a time gone by. It brings memories of a voice from his long, arduous life here in the hills and the prairie. It brings images of his ancestors in a day so long ago before he or his mother and father even existed – a vision of his family, two-leggeds and four-leggeds alike, mingling in peace, chasing after the buffalo to provide for the family, and running into battle to protect their way of life. He also feels a sense of mourning and loss that mingles with bravery and courage. It gives him pause. Midnight sees these things, all of them, and they have been carried to him on the prairie wind like a messenger telling him it is time. Time to go to the one who will help his kind find their people, their families, no matter the cost.

He gives a whinnying whistle to the flea-bitten lead mare to get the herd moving. She has a youngster at her side now, a feisty black colt with a white sock on his back leg. Her prominent hip bones and sway-back show her age, but she still manages to boss everyone around just fine. Midnight will let her retire soon and hopefully have the bay mare with white socks take over.

Frank's knees stiffen in his crouched position. He achingly rises and stretches his back. Maybe they've moved on. His intrusion has spooked them. Leo will know of some other places to catch sight of a wild herd.

He takes a deep breath and scans the valley once more. He can't explain what makes him stay – a pull from something that is so much bigger than him. The whispering voice he's heard and dismissed time and again hums in his ears. He knows it's not just the wind. It calls to him as it always does, but this time, among the sage and rocks and the sweeping hills and valleys, one word appears in his mind, clear as the sky above.

Purpose.

Then, he sees them. A small band of horses round the copse of cottonwoods. An old gray mare in the lead and a midnight-black stallion bringing up the rear.

The wind kicks up a notch as Leo comes loping up from the path holding his short-brimmed hat down. His shoes dangle from one hand. He slows as he sees the herd coming into view. He points to a stout blue roan. "See that one there? With all the scars? He's the alpha. He may be small, but he's in charge."

Midnight stands apart, ears erect and alert. The wind whips his mane in all directions. His liquid-black eyes and flaring nostrils are aimed directly at the brothers. His thick forelock bounces to the side as he watches over his band.

"I see him," says Frank as he catches his cowboy hat from the wind and seats it right back onto his head.

"That's a good-lookin' animal. My guess is he's been around a while."

Frank knows that his brother and their father have a good eye for horses, the best. They know exactly what to look for when it comes to conformation and whatnot, but he tends to doubt himself. People tell him what to look for, but it just doesn't register in his mind like it does for his brother and his dad. He simply hears, *Look at the horse's* this-n-that, or *Notice the delay between his* whatever, and *Do you see the slope of his* yadayadayada.

Frank looks at a horse and asks: Is it healthy? Hardy? Does she have good movement? Is he an athletic, sound son-of-a-bitch? For Frank, that's really what it all boils down to. This stud and his little band here tick all the boxes in Frank's book.

"Mmhm, they sure are." Frank's eyes are serious. "If we're looking to improve our bloodlines for the races, these horses are the ones to do it with. Just look at those bones. Those hooves! Have you ever seen a horse their size where the hoof is actually the right size for their body? These horses are," Leo pauses in search of the right words, "nature's perfection. I been doin' a lot of research, ya know, on these animals."

Frank keeps watching the horses interact with each other. "Yup," he says to Leo, "At the North Dakota State Historical Society's museums and centers. You've been spending a lot of time there." Frank notices an aging gray mare trot out to wrangle a couple of yearlings. Her ears go back and she sinks her head low like a dragon and weaves back and forth to get them back to a safer area closer to the rest. Leo is right about the black stallion being the alpha, but that mare, she's the boss.

Leo keeps going, "And you know I got those few from those ranchers a few years back. Then the couple I got from the round-ups after that, ya know."

"Yup," Frank says, still watching the horses interact with each other. "Bad Toe's a good horse."

"They all are. Jumping Mouse, Bald-faced Blue, Wolf Vixen, even Luppy. I tell ya, these horses have the lines our racers need, but the park still wants to get rid of 'em all."

They've had similar conversations to this many times before. The round-ups have been going on for years now, and neither of them like how the herds are handled out here. Some people claim that the park horses are pests, becoming inbred, or not pretty enough for the tourists, but these horses are wily adversaries. Local ranchers with sharp-shod horses would chase the native ponies over slippery-smooth rocky hillsides in the springtime. The riders would rope whatever they could but then set snares or set up hidden corral traps for the ones they couldn't. Even hunting them down with helicopters hasn't gotten the job done.

Frank knows these things. He does research himself. Despite it all, the horses are still here. They are survivors.

Leo says, "Ya, they sure do. I been watchin' at the round-ups too, Frank. They're targeting the most dominant native stallion." He nods at the black stallion who has determined it's safe enough to graze with a cautious eye. "I'm surprised this guy's still around."

Frank says, "He's one tough son-of-a-bitch."

"You know the park's brought in some domestic studs like a Shire bucking horse of all things, a Quarter Horse stallion, and some mares, and even an Arabian. Say they're gonna change the herd's genotype and phenotype. I suppose they're going to see if they can breed the Indian pony outta them." He doesn't know that for certain, but his gut tells him he's right.

Frank shakes his head. Again, he knows these things. This is not a new topic between the brothers. The thoughts get his blood pumping. It makes him want to do something about it. The park wants to alter these sound, strong, surviving native ponies' DNA by introducing a few domestic breeds. In Frank's mind, it's laughable. With these horses and their bloodlines, he and Leo would run circles around the cross-country race competition.

Leo's temper is brewing again, Frank can tell by the set of his jaw and the way he stares out at the herd. He decides not to add his fuel to it, so he sits down to watch the herd for a while. He can tell Leo knows he needs a moment too.

They watch how the horses move and interact with each other out in the tall grass. One heavy red roan mare dozes peacefully as a sparrow sits on her rump then flits away only to be replaced by another.

A gangly dun yearling wanders around looking for a good spot of grass. When she sneaks a little too close to an overo paint mare's claimed patch, she's met with pinned ears and bared teeth. She launches away having learned her lesson and goes to confide in the heavy but mellow red roan whose mouth is plum full of a fresh grab. The yearling breathes a heavy sigh as she yanks a few long blades sticking out of the red's mouthful. The red roan maintains her lowered head and contentedly munches away.

A young, black foal with a white sock lifts his head groggily. When he realizes his mother is no longer close by, he pops up on his gangly legs and searches for her. He whinnies urgently, but the sound carries in the wrong direction. His gray mother, the boss mare, has meandered far in the other direction to graze and keep a watchful eye on the rambunctious older, blue roan colts. One is bigger than the other, and their "play" looks more like a fight than just "bite, bite, kick." Frank imagines that big one will be on his own soon enough, off to find a bachelor band until he can claim some mares of his own, unless the round-ups get him first.

The baby whinnies a little more frantically and starts to awkwardly run in one direction, then the next. Another mare, a bay, goes to him and tries to nuzzle him calmly, comfort him, but he is having nothing of it. He wants his mother!

At this point, the alpha stallion raises his head proudly and confidently and strides over to the youngster. He stands, head high in the wind, over the baby and releases a clarion blast that slices through the prairie wind, making the gray mare pop her head up in his direction. He sounds his alarm again and stomps his mighty leg two times. The mare comes jogging over to her baby. She consoles him as he nuzzles in close to her familiar smell and warmth.

The blue stallion dips his head to them and murmurs approvingly. Then he moves off to graze on his own again.

As Frank watches this whole scene play out before him, he sees such a unique beauty in the way these animals interact and communicate with each other. Oh, he knows all horse herds have an order and way of getting their points across to one another, but watching this little band really makes him think.

These rustic, hairy, compact animals truly have a unique social structure and language of their own. They understand each other, clear as day. They take care of each other, look out for one another. The compassion they show is palpable. It kicks Frank right in the gut.

It's not right. These are not some feral horses running wild. To think anyone would call them ugly, like that's a perfectly rational reason to destroy an entire bloodline. Anyone who takes the time to truly see them – see how they are, how they talk, how they play, how they live together as a family – would realize how unique they are.

In this moment, unexpectedly, Frank can't block out the visions of war, nor the injustices he witnessed. The rotten things he said and did under horrible influences flood his mind. He sees the innocent people in the simple villages blown to bits and remembers the Vietnamese mother crying inconsolably on the curb as she rocked the pieces of her broken baby.

Someone should have stood up for her. Someone should have said something and deep down, Frank knows that someone could have been him. The past is the past. He made choices and he has to live with them. What he does now is what matters.

He listens to the nickers and sighs and snorts and squeals that play on the wind. Someone needs to speak for these horses before it's too late.

Frank finally says to Leo, who has settled down and is chewing on a blade of grass, "we need to get as many as we can from the round-up auctions."

A glint of fire lights Leo's eyes. "They'll be cheap, ya know. They'll mostly be slotted for the can. We won't have to pay more 'n a penny over the kill price."

Frank's wheels are turning. "We'll get a loan. Well, we'll get *you* a loan. I doubt the bank would give me a dime what with my own mortgage and debt already."

Leo says, "We'll recoup some of what we spend in winnings at the races." The hope in his voice is evident.

Frank nods but feels hesitant to get too excited just yet. "We'll buy what we can, and we'll take 'em home."

Leo suggests, "Would the wife be okay with ya heading into town for a beer so we can talk details?"

"You kidding? Maria will have my hide." He shakes his head. "But this needs to get done." He looks out at the horses as they turn to leave. "Those horses need us as much as we need them." He looks down the path leading away and says, "let's do something about it."

Chapter 10
Rain

We should be as water, which is lower than all things yet stronger even than the rocks.
~ Oglala Lakota Sioux Proverb

2023 - 4:52 AM

One might think it's the rumbling thunder or the nonstop pouring rain that wakes Frank. Possibly, it is his own creaking bones in the damp June air.

It's not.

It's the ponies.

They are always on his mind. They have been for over 40 years. Today is no different. Yet, it is different. It's all different now.

Rain thrums the old roof, and an aching chill threads from Frank's thoughts straight into his core. He can't hold still anymore. He doesn't want to wake Shelly, lying next to him, as she has as his wife for the last 30 years. Her tiny snores burble daintily, and he smiles softly at her slumber. At least she can sleep.

The floor is cold beneath his bare feet as he slips them into his worn slippers and quietly gets into jeans and a button-up plaid shirt. He grabs his cheaters from the nightstand and hangs them around his neck.

Coffee.

He makes his way past the jungle of houseplants and through the living room. He nudges the sleeping body on the couch.

"Time to get up, Justice," Franks whispers.

An obligatory affirmative groan is all the reply he gets from Justice, Jennifer's son. Frank leaves the boy alone for now. He'll be needing his young back today. Might as well give him a few minutes more rest.

Jennifer moved back down south with her daughter and new grandbaby. Frank simply could not afford to pay her, so it was her call. She took her bottle-fed mare, Annabelle, in a rickety old trailer and hauled back to where she used to call home. It's been tough without her. From the day he took her in – when she needed someone to save her from herself – Jenn had been his right hand with the ranch. It's taking some getting-used-to not having her around.

At least Justice is able to stay until he's done with school. Frank is thankful for that. Not just for the extra help. To Frank, the boy is family.

Out the window, a flicker of lightning illuminates his way to the kitchen. At the table, he counts out his handful of pills while the coffee brews. This one for this. That one for that. These for before he eats. Those for after. A veritable pharmaceutical buffet.

Cancer. What a bitch.

Although his numbers have been creeping up for a while lately, he has no intention of going back for yet another round of treatment, like the doctors want him to. He simply can't sacrifice the time it takes to drive back and forth to Bismarck for appointments. Plus, the treatments always make him feel like shit. Same old, same old. Ever since he came back from the war, he and Leo were the same. Thank you, Agent Orange.

Today, he will wait to go over to the ranch. His and Shelly's place in town is a reprieve from the mess over there. This rain just will not stop. Of course, Frank will never be mad about rain – he's gone too many North Dakota summers without it – but this much over the last weeks is really making things difficult to manage out at the farm.

His leg involuntarily starts to bounce anxiously as he thinks about it. That's all he's done lately. Too much time to think.

Nearly 200 horses standing out there in it, day in and day out. His broken-down machinery is driving him nuts, not to mention all the parts and repairs he needs but can't afford. The words *robbed* and *used* litter his thoughts daily. To think, some people on the board are millionaires. They have been benefiting from the Nokota horse since 1999, but he is left with nothing. They have taken away his life like thieves!

The guilt he feels for yelling at Justice and his nephew Logan for the dumbest, little things lately makes him wipe a hand over his face. Thank the maker they're here. They're young and strong, and they're willing to work in exchange for a place to live with people who appreciate and love them. It's just that the hopelessness, some days, consumes him. Dark thoughts threaten to force his hand and throw in the towel on the whole damn thing. He doesn't need this. He could live a life with just his few saddle horses and a few mares. Enough's enough. All he has to do is say, "Okay. Take my horses," and let the herd go.

Even the thought of the words tastes like bile in his throat.

The weight of his promise to the horses flows over him like a river. He told them he would speak for them. He promised to take care of them until he found a way to get them back to their people or at least give them a place to live as nature intended.

He takes his last pill with a long drink of water, closes his eyes, and inhales deeply. When he opens them, he shoves up from the table, pours a travel mug of coffee, and rouses Justice from the couch.

The quick drive to Frank's little farm just outside of Linton goes by in a blink. He could do it with his eyes closed. Justice's eyes *are* closed, but Frank doesn't say anything.

His stomach clenches as he drives past the landowner's prairie that runs along the highway. At least the horses aren't up on the hill this morning.

Anxiety threatens to force his pills back into his throat as he approaches his farm. He feels sick about his ponies living in this tight space. In the muck and the manure and mud. God, if this rain could just let up.

Rolling down the muddy driveway is more like skiing. At least the trench they dug down its center is working, a little, to route the flow of water away from the pens.

Rain batters the windshield. Even the wipers on full speed don't help. The truck lurches this way and that until eventually they slide to a stop on a somewhat grassy spot near the machine shed.

He sees the porch light come on. The old house came with the property when Frank bought it. He's always had a ranch hand living in it, but it's kind of run down. Then Frank built the little cabin behind it for himself. This way, he can have his own space on all the long days he spends out here. As long as he has someone he trusts live in the house and watch over the horses, Frank is fine with going back and forth to town every day and night to live in the comfort of his and Shelly's home.

Logan is up. Good. Logan is family, and the young man stepped up when he heard Frank and the horses needed help, so he moved in after Jenn left. It's been good to have someone fixing up the house a little. He's got to help move panels today with Justice. How they're going to stay upright in this sludge is beyond him.

The sound of the drumming rain seems to let up just a hair, so all three make a break for the machine shed.

"Whew!" Justice says. "It's really coming down!"

Logan shakes his hair and swipes the water off his jacket. "I gotta say, I'm full-on sick of it."

Frank says, "I hate to complain about rain. There's nothing we can do about it."

Justice agrees and says, "Let's get it done." He starts out the shop door.

"Hang on," says Logan, "I got us these at the hardware store. They were up by the registers. Clearance. .50 apiece." He reaches into his hoodie pocket and tosses Frank and Justice a plastic poncho, the thin kind that comes in the little plastic pouches.

Frank catches his yellow pocket poncho and says, "Save it for yourselves. I'll be in the cab." Then he gives them a *ha-ha* sneer and takes off outside to climb into the tractor.

The two boys just smile and shake their heads as they slip their purple and orange slickers over their heads. They only reach to just below their butts. At least they'll be dry, sort of.

The New Holland's engine rumbles to life. Frank starts moving the first several rounds. The massive tires ooze fairly easily through the mud. It's a good tractor, especially for being over 20 years old. If only he could get the blasted PTO working.

The boys trudge as fast as they can to open the gate to the mares. Their Muck boots get sucked in like quicksand with every step. Step, lift, suck. Step, lift, suck.

The mares all turn with perked ears at the bale coming in. They wait patiently for Frank to set it down on the slant. The boys cut the twine off and help unroll it down the slope. The mares move in to enjoy their breakfast. Frank backs out, and the boys close the gate. Off they go to do the same for the stud pen, and then the hard keepers, the young ones, and of course his saddle horses.

The routine of it lends some meager sense of comfort or at the very least, assurance. Considering how hard the winter had been on them, underneath all the mud and shedding coats, the horses look pretty good.

All things considered, feeding goes quickly, and before he knows it, Frank is sitting inside his little cabin. He will head back to town soon and have breakfast with Shelly, and he'll wait for the best part of his day – his morning FaceTime visit with his grandsons. For now, he sits at the little wooden table in the center of the room, has a cup of coffee and a cigarette, and watches the rain keep coming down over the tiny slice of prairie he still gets to enjoy. The sliding glass doors have rivulets running down like tears, but the view is all the more beautiful for it. It's not his prairie, but at least he can see it. It's been hard watching the prairie disappear. The geese, ducks, and cranes are fewer in number these days because of it. It's the meadowlarks he's missing the most.

He thinks about how easy it used to be to find ground around here to hay. Not anymore. Just like back when he had to travel all over Kingdom Come to find hay for the horses, he's once again hard-pressed to find places that will let him put up quality prairie grass for his horses.

The thought of haying sends a ripple of stress through him. He's got to figure out how to get that PTO on the tractor fixed. That'll be expensive. Then again, this rain has to stop at some point if anything is going to dry out enough to even cut a single blade. He'll put up wet hay if he has to. The horses go through it so fast that it won't have time to grow mildew or mold anyway.

He shakes the thoughts of things he can't control just now out of his head and mashes his cigarette into the ashtray.

Time to check the phone.

Frank snaps his two-piece, magnetic cheaters on and scrolls through his phone to see what drama Facebook has for him today. He's not afraid of a fight – he has nothing but truths to tell – but he's sick of some of the crap he sees on his phone.

One day he'd seen a car drive by super-slowly, stay a few seconds, then squeal off like a bank robber. Then later, someone posted some grainy, ultra-zoomed-in pictures of a few of his mares. The pictures made it look like he was starving his horses to death with squaller and neglect. That was one of the shittiest moves he'd seen yet. Of course, *that* got all sorts of people up in arms.

Thank God Christa has a handle on the replies that go out to everyone out there who has an opinion on everything. She created an entirely new website for the Kuntz Nokota Ranch, made a cool new logo to represent them with their Z4 brand, and got the word out to thousands on all those new-fangled platforms or whatever you call them. She reacts and replies diplomatically and truthfully, but never takes the low road that some attackers do. He's glad to let her handle the idiots out there. When she finds time to do it all, with two jobs and two little boys? He has no idea. The kid's amazing. All his daughters are.

He needs some time to get his feet under him. Get a handle on things, not just figure out where his next load of hay is going to come from.

He goes back to the home screen and sees a little 1 in a red circle on his voicemail icon and wonders whose call he missed. He looks down his nose at it and taps it. The voicemail message screen shows, and he pushes the play triangle button.

Someone wants to donate hay again.

Then he sees a 12 in a little red circle on his email icon. He taps that and opens an email notification from the GoFundMe fundraiser Christa set up a while ago to help with expenses for the horses. More and more donations keep coming in, some 20 bucks, others a lot more.

At this, he feels something inside his heart lift, and his anger softens. He will never get used to the fact that so many people – some he's never even met – really do care about his Nokota and the predicament they are in. He can't quite get over that feeling when they reach out to him. It's humbling to see how many people out there want to help his horses. They send him their hard-earned money, knowing he will give it all to the herd.

They believe in him.

That's enough to keep him fighting another day.

Chapter 11
Shifting Winds

Listen to the wind, it talks. Listen to the silence, it speaks. Listen to your heart, it knows.
~ Native American Proverb

Still 1984-86
Theodore Roosevelt National Park

The introduction of domesticated stallions is underway. Arabians and Quarter Horses are two breed types brought into the park. The idea is that these studs will dominate the native stallions and acquire their mares so that their domesticated genetics will infiltrate and alter the genotype and phenotype of the native horses. This initiative is intended to change all that the native horses are, molding them into what some people believe they should be.

Midnight's band is not safe from the domestic invaders.

* * *

Riding on a gust, the evening's waning prairie winds sweep Midnight's heavy forelock from his eyes. He snorts hard so that mist shoots out his red, flared nostrils. The scent of a new stallion lights his senses afire. On the slope just ahead stands a slender, long-legged stallion whose entire glossy body shudders as he trumpets a challenge. The intruder flings his refined head then raises his tail high as a wispy cloud while he high-step prances back and forth, inching his way closer to Midnight's herd. The stallion brings with him the dry, arid air of desert places, of endless sun and sands. The wide-set, shiny-black eyes convey his intent. He is here for the mares.

Midnight stands strong – as still as the rocky hillside behind him. One ear flicks to his mares, while the other remains pricked toward the intruder. Only the rapid rise and fall of the other horse's ribs reveals his anticipation of a fight. Midnight gives a sharp, guttural command, and the gray lead mare begins nudging the herd away from the impending scuffle and into a huddle position.

The gray mare can tell this newcomer is going to be no match for her alpha. That flightiness, the inexperience, this horse is clearly not from around here. He won't have a chance of winning them over.

Just like the one that challenged her alpha a few moons ago...

That stranger – the color of earth – already had four or five mares of his own. Those mares had indeed been her kind too. The sturdy legs, feathers cascading down hardy hooves, low-set tails, and roany coloring – they shared ancestors. This was reassuring, aside from the fact that the invader was here to take more for himself. It had been so long since Midnight's little band had seen others of their kind. She and her alpha had nearly lost hope that there even *were* more. The earth-brown intruder, definitely *not* one of her ancestors, had them!

She recalls that brown horse's encounter. That had been an interesting fight. He'd had a way of spinning quickly on his massive, meaty hindquarters. He had dodged and weaved in a way Midnight had not experienced. Midnight, her beloved alpha, adapted quickly to his brown opponent's strategies and soon enough sent him packing with one less mare than he'd arrived with.

Midnight, too, wonders where these new stallions are coming from. How are they getting here? Why have they invaded his home? More importantly, why are they threatening to take his family from him?

This white, springy stallion before them now has no apparent strategy. Thievery is all he is thinking about. Suddenly the white stallion springs forward at such a blinding pace that Midnight's eyes widen for just a second. Midnight's bulging muscles ripple beneath his ebony coat. Then he lowers his head and paws the ground once.

The white stallion devours the ground between them. His slender legs pound thunder into the earth.

Midnight paws twice.

The thief reaches out his head like an ancient bird of prey. Razor-sharp teeth glint in the last rays of sunlight. The wild whites of his eyes sear into the black stud, attempting to strike fear in the older stallion.

Midnight strikes the earth a third time and risks a glance at his band to make sure they are safe. They whinny nervously but stay together. The black foal with the half sock squirts out of the formation, but the lead mare nips at him gently to get him back to safety.

When only two lengths remain between them, Midnight rears up to his full height to meet his foe head-on. On first impact, he can tell that his mass outweighs this stud, even though Midnight is smaller in stature. One strike of his front feet slashes into the glossy white shoulder and knocks him off balance, stunning the other stallion for a second. Crimson blood, stark against the white coat, trickles down his shoulder. His nostrils flare wild as the wind carries the black stallion's mares' scents to him, reminding him of his purpose here.

Blocking the pain in his shoulder, the white stud flies at Midnight. Their bodies bash against each other and they push with all their force. In one twisting motion, the white stallion somehow wrenches his neck in a most unnatural way to slice at his opponent's neck. Midnight feels the raking teeth at his throat and lets out a piercing scream. This foe might not have a strategy, but he makes up for it with wild fury. Flecks of foam splatter from the horse's mouth, showing he is tiring.

Deciding this fight needs to end now, Midnight whirls around with lightning speed. Both his back legs punch through the air, landing squarely on the thief's barrel and injured shoulder over and over again.

The white horse rears and lashes his hooves to no avail at the relentless onslaught. His instincts tell him to stay and fight to the death, but the pain tells him it is time to flee. He will come back another day, refreshed and more knowledgeable. He spins on his haunches and heads for the hills from which he came. He stumbles but regains balance and maintains speed.

Midnight chases after him for a stretch. He knows this prairie ground – each gopher hole and rocky patch. If he wanted to, he could run the white stallion down and make him pay dearly for trying to steal his mares and make sure he never comes back. But he feels this fight is over. He has won. He has deeply humbled his opponent and earned a new scar. There is no need for more violence. So he drops back, snorts good riddance, and makes a wide arching victory circle over his domain back to his herd.

* * *

Still 1984-86
Leo and Pauline Kuntz's Homestead, Linton, ND

Frank and Brother Leo Kuntz hang over the wooden corral watching the horses. Their father rests his square shoulders on the rails with them. The look in Leo Kuntz's eyes is as tough to read as it has been all of Frank's life. It's either skeptical or mildly impressed. Either way, Frank is thankful his parents are willing to house the few horses they've collected from the park so far. He keeps a watchful eye on his girls riding their ponies into the creek out back. Their laughter is a familiar, welcome backdrop to what could end up being an awkward conversation among the men. He hears Alecia let out a shriek of terror, and his instinct tells him to run to her, but then he hears Dawn laughing and sees her get off her horse to go pull a leech off her sister's leg.

Dawn's sweet voice carries on the wind, "Race ya!" He sees her leap back onto her pony's back and take off like a shot over a long, grassy stretch. Alecia, always game for fast fun, yips at her pony and takes off after her sister without a care. Their dog Blue chases after them through the tall grass, barking at the joy of it all.

Frank cannot wait to watch their baby sister Christa join them out there someday. He's sure their Maria will appreciate it too, so she won't have to take care of the little munchkin at the video store. Usually, Dawn and Alecia babysit their little sister while Mommy works. He chuckles inwardly at the image of Alecia pushing crazy-pigtailed Christa around in that stroller that is twice her size up and down the block in Linton. With Dawn being the motherly, fiercely protective big sister – what with a nine-year age gap – and Alecia's natural ability and desire to soothe any hurt or comfort anything a toddler finds worthy of tears, they were indispensable sidekicks.

Today, however, Frank had offered a pony ride at Grandma and Grandpa's, and that is always impossible to turn down.

Frank and Leo hear the screen door on the house bang and see their mother Pauline hang her apron on a nail and walk out to the corral to stand next to her husband. She has a brief moment in between meals where she can come out and be a part of the conversation. Watching Frank's girls play is always a welcome reprieve from her long day of work on the farm. Though she typically sees the horses as just another job that has to be done, she can't help herself when she watches these park horses move.

Pauline slowly shakes her head and tsk-tsks. "They certainly are beautiful creatures, yes they are." She tucks a long strand of hair that the breeze has playfully tugged out of her bun behind her ear. She watches the one Leo calls Bad Toe parade around with a flowing action that looks like he's prancing through water.

"The big round-up is still coming up." Brother Leo says breaking into Frank's thoughts. "Next year, I'm hearing. In the spring probably. We got to be ready for that one."

"Ya," Leo says, "Ya need numbers to diversify your herd."

It's humid and buggy, but a late-summer breeze riffles through the pen. Frank shoves his hands in his pockets. His father hasn't said too much about these horses they've gotten from the park so far, but Frank knows that his dad knows horses. He is certain – whether he shows it or not – that his dad is impressed with these animals.

Frank says, "I, uh, you know I've got that loan I'm trying to pay off. The interest rates just keep going up."

"Uh huh," says his father as he zeroes in on a speedy little black stud.

Frank eyes his brother, who for some reason will not make eye contact with him right now. So he keeps going. "So ... my place can't handle the numbers we're planning for. If, um, things go how we're hoping, I don't know if I'll have room for very many."

A long stretch of silence goes by. Frank starts to wonder if he maybe shouldn't have brought it up.

Their dad points to the little black stud playing around in the pen with the others. He says, "Just look at that quick little devil go."

Brother Leo chimes in immediately, "Yup. Quick as shit. He can maintain it too. These horses, Dad, they're made for cross-country running. They're *doing* horses."

Another gust of wind blasts through their conversation. Frank agrees, of course, about the horses being made for the races. In fact, the three men have already determined that they won't need to do much cross-breeding, if any. Maybe they could cross some with the ponies for the carriage rides, but these horses are designed as perfect as can be.

Something digs at him deep down and keeps telling him these horses are – he searches his mind for the right words – that their purpose here is so much more important. He wants to speak up and tell his dad about how these horses have a unique language among each other. He'd like to say something about their special social structure and ability to show compassion like no domesticated breed he's ever known. He's just not sure how receptive their father will be to the thought of supporting their horses based on emotions.

Instead, he goes a different route. "Leo," Frank says to his brother, "Tell Dad about the research you've been doing."

"Naw, you know about as much as me," he says. "You go ahead."

"Sure, but the stuff you found at the State Historical Society Center. That goes way back."

Their dad pipes in to cut their arguing, like when they were kids, "I'm listening. Both of you, go on."

* * *

History Lesson

In 1876 Sitting Bull, the great Hunkpapa Lakota warrior and chief, led his people as well as the Cheyenne and Arapaho to victory by annihilating Lieutenant Colonel George Armstrong Custer and all the men under his command at the Battle of the Little Bighorn, known to the Hunkpapa Lakota as Battle of Greasy Grass. As Sitting Bull soon realized, he now had the full wrath of the United States military to deal with.

Eventually, under the threat of starvation, he led his remaining followers into Canada, hoping to find a welcome refuge. The Canadian government, however, did not find it their responsibility to take in and feed people whose reservation was south of the border.

After struggling to survive for four years, famine finally drove Sitting Bull and his last holdouts to cross back into the United States, where they surrendered to the authorities at Fort Buford in North Dakota. Once they were placed on their reservations, the cavalry was sent to round up and confiscate their horses to discourage their mobility. They insisted their assignment was under the premise that the *native-type* horses carried diseases. The small, rough-looking horses with odd coat colors were either shot or sent to auctions where traders would sell them through public sales.

Here enters the Marquis de Mores from France. Being a man of aristocratic background and exceptional knowledge about horses, this expert horseman saw something quite different than the locals saw. He admired the horses' story and their stamina, so much so that he bought 250 of them for himself from the Fort Buford traders.

This extravagant entrepreneur and his American-born wife, Medora, had chosen the Little Missouri Badlands for their dream of creating a cattle empire. They built a luxurious home, bought the finest stock facilities money could buy, complete with a packing plant, and founded the town of Medora.

De Mores and his wife were superior riders and well-versed in horsemanship. They were also able to see the valuable qualities in these so-called "Indian ponies," so they began breeding their own Lakota herd.

In 1884, the Marquis de Mores sold 60 of these horses to A.C. Huidekoper, another entrepreneur who owned a massive horse breeding enterprise that would eventually become the largest in North Dakota. He developed some of the first (and very popular) Percherons for farming and driving. He was always looking for ways to create the perfect horse, and he found these Indian horses were excellent for crossbreeding, particularly with his Thoroughbreds and Percherons. He gave them his Z4 brand and called them "American horses." He then sold them as saddle horses, racehorses, and even polo ponies.

As most big ranchers did back in this era, both De Mores and Huidekoper "range-bred" much of their stock, meaning they fed their stock on unfenced rangeland, the Badlands. When De Mores' operation went under in the winter of 1886, many of his horses, it is believed, went on to contribute to wild bands.

When Huidekoper ceased operating in the early 20th century, the horses he was unable to recover remained on the range. Only the wiliest, the strongest, and smartest were able to evade recapture. Decades later, residents said his horses were still there or in the hands of ranchers.

During the Great Depression, many of the feral horses in the park were also branded ranch horses whose owners had used the park as a grazing commons. Repossessed horses were let loose in the park as well. So, in the late 1940s and 50s, when the Theodore Roosevelt National Park fenced this area, these remaining horses were inadvertently enclosed. The 1954 round-up was meant to remove all the horses and get them back to their ranchers. Of the 125 brought in, 99% of them had ranch brands. Again, the 1% that could not be recovered, were the strongest, bravest, and smartest - the native bred ponies.

Frank punctuates the end with, "And just like back in the 40s and 50s, they're rounding the native horses up again, trying to exterminate them all. They're shooting them. Rounding them up with helicopters. And why?" He notices his voice is a little louder and higher-pitched than he means for it to be, but he can't stop himself. "They call 'em a 'nuisance' or they're not *pretty enough* for the tourists! Ugh!" He throws his hands in the air, turns to lean on the rail, and with a clenched jaw, stares at the horses in the pen and then out at his children on their pony ride. This is not the kind of world he wants his girls to grow up in.

There is quiet for a moment, then Brother Leo kicks the dirt with his bare foot, shoves his hands in his pockets, and says, "I bet if they'd been Custer's horses, it'd be a different story."

Frank's mind is far away drifting through the pages of the cowboys and Indians books of his childhood – images of natives fighting fiercely with primitive weapons against guns and cannons. Then his mind is catapulted ahead to the war-torn villages of Vietnam, the dirty, motherless children, and vacant, hopeless faces.

His voice is quiet now as he says, "I know it'll be a challenge, but I guess," he shifts his weight onto his other leg, "we're hoping somewhere down the road, somebody will realize what a potential treasure this breed is."

Leo adds, "then maybe the park will want them back. You know, once they see what they really are."

Frank finishes with, "we just can't continue to throw things away all the time, or let it get destroyed."

Their father and mother have been quiet this whole time. Pauline rests a hand on her husband's shoulder and they both give each other an understanding look.

Frank knows that no self-respecting German is going to take a risk on something that isn't well worth it. He and his brother both know these horses are worth it. Whether for cross-breeding or something bigger – bigger than what he can even wrap his head around yet. The truth is, they need their parents' help if they're going to do this. The horses need the land.

Leo Kuntz looks at his sons. He straightens from the corral rail he's been leaning on the entire time. His brow carries a severe crease and his wrinkles emphasize the downward curve of his mouth. He looks at his wife, takes a deep breath, and looks back at his sons. Finally, matter-of-factly, he says, "we have room," and walks off to the barn to work on the tractor.

Chapter 12
1986 Round-Up

Let us put our minds together and see what we can make for our children.
~ Sitting Bull

1986
Theodore Roosevelt National Park

Electricity charges the air. Midnight's whole herd is agitated. Even the up-and-coming stallions collect close by him, stone still, watching the hills. The big blue roan and the smaller one have moved on from his herd and the new youngsters know this is not time for play. Midnight knows that one of them will have to take over at some point, but today, they look to him for leadership. There is a nervous hum in the earth, in the trees, in the birds soaring overhead.

Something is hunting them, and it is not another stallion or any prey animal.

Midnight inhales deeply and his body quivers at the scents he finds in the wind. Two-leggeds, many of them, on unfamiliar horses. The iron bird with bug eyes. The increasing intensity sends the herd into a frenzy. The old gray lead mare, her black colt with one white sock still at her side, starts them all moving. Midnight knows it's the right thing to do. He delivers an earsplitting whistle command to follow her. A younger red roan stud, however, refuses to turn and run. Instead, he lurches forward, ready to meet his foe head-on like he has seen his alpha do time and time again without fear or hesitation.

The smaller blue roan stud, already following orders to flee, falters as he realizes his brother has stayed. He slides to a hard stop, wheels around, and joins him in pursuit of the oncoming enemy.

Midnight screams at them to join the band, but they have made up their minds, so he too wheels and races toward them to help. The lead mare sweeps the herd in a wide arc, buying time. She suddenly sees what the stallions are up against. What is coming for them all.

Breaching the wide horizon is a long line of horses with two-leggeds astride them. The earth rumbles. There are so many. Wild yips and haws, pops, and snaps crackle over the prairie.

Behind them, like an iron moon rising slowly into the sky, is the bug-eyed machine that has chased them before. Its *whup-whup-whup* drowns out all other sounds of the pursuers.

Midnight, running stride for stride next to the younger studs, sees it all and knows from experience that they cannot fight this enemy. He surges ahead a few lengths and forces the other two to turn and flee. It is their only chance. The two studs fling their heads and strike out in defiance, but eventually, they succumb to his absolute authority and angle away.

Midnight follows.

They run. The old, the weak, the young, they all run. Over the hills, through the trees, along the river. The sun travels across the sky, their foes never stop chasing, never stop pressing.

Midnight realizes now that his herd is being pushed, not hunted. If one falls out of the group, the two-leggeds on horses chase them down and seem to try to get them back into formation.

The pace is so fast. The terrain is so rugged. They've been running so long.

The gray mare is still keeping pace with her youngster close by. Her nostrils are streaked with blood as are several others'. Their bodies are drenched with sweat. Blue roans look solid black. Foam spatters like pink and white dirt and drips down their legs. Their lungs ache as they heave in and out demanding their next breath. No one whinnies. No one screams or cries anymore. All their reserves are channeled for survival.

After what will be the longest race of their lives, they come upon an open, flat space where more two-leggeds wait. Those chasing them intensify their effort and begin to close in on the herd's flanks. Several of his family stumble, trample each other, and fall. Some do not get up. Midnight's eyes go wide, and he tries to cry out to them, but he has no air left to give. If he stops for them, he might not get back up either.

There are heavy fences ahead, enclosures. Two-leggeds on horses are positioned on either side of the openings, and immediately, the seasoned stallion knows this is a trap.

He must decide now. Does he allow his herd to be captured? Does he simply let them go through the opening to whatever end?

The gray mare up ahead has already made her decision. She and her black colt veer sharp and dodge every onslaught the enemy attempts on her. Her old bones rattle as she somehow evades them. She is so, so tired, but her black colt follows with lightning speed, agile as a fox, so she fights on for him.

Midnight decides she is right. He will fight for his herd. He must fight one last time for their freedom.

Time and Earth pause. The alpha stallion slows his pace and lets the rest scatter ahead. The horses with riders fly past in pursuit of the others, their collected mob now turned to chaos. With immense dignity and the mightiest sense of control, he turns around – drenched mane and tail slashing like bloodied whips across his body, black as a starless night – to face the enemy.

Whup-whup-whup-whup-whup.

Midnight rises to his full height, slices the air with his hooves, and releases a maniacal death cry that no other horse has ever rivaled since. The aircraft hovers in front of him. It sinks lower and lower, trying to push him toward the pen. This is a fight between metal against flesh and bone and the power of his ancestors. He hears their voices echoing in his war-torn ears. They are here, here with him, with his family. He must believe this. He does believe this. That is what launches him in the air straight at the flying contraption. Its spinning blades slice a hair's breadth from his head. He throws his body into unnatural contortions in an attempt to strike it with a bone-crushing kick.

When he crashes to the ground, he then realizes he cannot defeat this foe.

For a moment, he finds his breath. His eyes catch sight, just beneath the belly of the metal beast, of a copse of sage and cottonwood trees in the distance. It's not that far away. If he could just run that stretch. *This, he thinks, is either my chance to escape or to meet my maker and rejoin my people in the spirit world.*

It is not his time. The machine hovers low, very low. The two-leggeds inside stare wide-eyed at him as he gauges how much space is between him and freedom. The flying machine wobbles uneasily as if watching him curiously. He lifts his head in defiance one last time then takes off like a shot straight for its underbelly. He stretches his neck out, long, and low, like a bird of prey, streaks underneath, and shoots out the back toward the trees. Then the machine tips and nearly comes crashing down. It regains balance and flies away.

Not able to quite believe it's gone, Midnight strains to run with every last ounce of strength he can muster. When the sound of the machine lessens, he slows down to look toward the others. They still fight, and he is proud to have been their leader all these years.

Then a strange sense comes over him as he looks at a few of the two-leggeds standing apart from the chasers. They have their hands to their eyes as they squint into the sun. They see him. Even after all he has been through, despite the sweat and blood dripping down his sides, and even though he carries a red-hot hatred for his enemies, he senses something from the ones watching him now. He exhales long and hard, then turns to make his way to the copse of trees not far in the distance. With him flows the knowledge that someone will look after his herd now that he can't.

He feels it like the promise of spring after the death-cold of winter.

Someone will keep fighting for his family.

* * *

"What kind of a shit show are you running here!" Frank rages at a park official after watching the black-as-night stallion escape back into the wild. "These guys may be good riders, but they're causing nothing but chaos out there!" Frank is well aware that his brothers Leo and Joe are two of those riders, but he knows his brothers are not like the rest of these men. "Look at 'em! Running that old gray mare? Why? And those idiots over there, bullying that big stud trying to get outta the pens? You can't use a cattle prod on horses! They're tormenting him."

The stud tries again and again to jump out of the pen, and the men around him poke and prod and laugh at him, calling him *dog food*."

This stout blue roan is from Midnight's band, and he is fighting like his alpha had shown him growing up all those years. He is an alpha now himself, with his own large band of mares and foals. He will do whatever it takes to get free. To survive. The men keep jabbing him with the biting stick, and it is taking its toll on his spirit.

Frank flings his arms at the shoddily arranged corral panels. "This whole operation is ridiculous! Look at that! Who in their right mind would pen up more than one band together?"

Two studs rear up to fight each other.

"The foals are getting trampled!"

His entire world is full of exclamation marks as he witnesses this brutal scene. The disorganization, harshness, and sheer chaos was mind-boggling. Egos rule over humanity here. Frank manages to contain his anger. His pent-up rage forces him to pace and seek out anyone who will listen to reason. There's a woman going around with a video camera, and she's got a 35mm hanging on her shoulder too. By the things she's choosing to catch on tape (and the strands of hair stuck to tear streaks on her cheeks), Frank can guess pretty well she's disgusted with the ordeal too.

"Listen, Frank," one official tries to placate him. "These guys know what they're doing. They're the best ranchers in the area. Who knows how we would've rounded this many up if it weren't for them? Besides, these *parkies* are mostly going to the can anyway."

Frank bristles at that – the blatant disregard for life. "Well, that lady over there's been videotaping the whole debacle. She don't look too happy about all this."

The park official is well aware of the woman with the camera. "She's working for the park. That's a park service camera she's got there." He knows she isn't happy with what's happening out here. This park official, however, doesn't feel the need to let Frank Kuntz know that.

Frank, not waiting for whatever reply this guy is going to try to make up, says, "I just hope she takes it to the news. All of it." He turns his back on the official.

Frank feels like he's about to be sick. He hasn't felt this way since the last time he went deer hunting shortly after coming back from Vietnam. He had grown up hunting. The Kuntz men hunt, provide for the family, yada-yada-yada, but that last time, he shot and wounded a little buck. It took off, so Frank went to track it down. He never found it. All he could think was, *That poor animal had to suffer because of my mistake. We're supposed to* protect *life, not* take *it.* That's when he decided he wasn't going to hunt again.

He hears the heart-wrenching moan of the old gray mare calling out over the corral panels for someone, trying to find her youngster. Then he shields his eyes from the sun and squints toward the helicopter trying to nab a small black stallion.

In disbelief – although not totally, because Frank has seen these horses do some amazing things here today – Frank watches the black-as-night stallion turn to face the helicopter head-on! To think of the *courage* that takes. Then, as if *that* isn't enough, he sees the horse launch, from what have to be exhausted legs after that twenty-mile chase they all endured, toward the low-hovering machine. Frank's heart clenches at how close the animal comes to decapitating itself. Then, like some ninja movie, the stud stretches his body out like a dragon and streaks right under the helicopter.

The look of alarm on the faces of the guys in the chopper spoke volumes. Frank looks down at his boots to hide what might have been a laugh. The pilot tries to pull up, but he's sunk too low, so the helicopter wobbles and darned near crashes. After a moment, and once the little midnight-black stallion is well on his way to a copse of trees, the chopper regains balance and moves toward the pens.

Frank takes a moment to honor such a brave warrior who defeated an impossible foe. Again, he feels empathy and deep respect for the Lakota people of this homeland he loves so much. How they went up against the impossible foe – the U.S. military – and, at the Battle of Greasy Grass at least, were victorious.

With eyes already creased too much from life, Frank watches the stallion go, wondering where he will go now. Frank's breath catches in his chest. To his surprise, he sees the horse standing, looking right back at him. Though there is quite a great distance between them, somehow, Frank knows this stallion is indeed straight-on looking *at him*. The prairie wind connects them in spirit.

This whole day of violence, pain, fear, and chaos makes his stomach sick. He turns his head and watches how valiantly the captured ones fight. How they all tirelessly demand their freedom. How they so badly want to *live*. It's so sad how with people like the ones here today, that will never happen. They want to change the park horses, replace them, and make them into something palatable for public perception. Change their genotype and phenotype so they are no longer what they are.

The humans will get what they want unless someone fights back, unless someone speaks up. He looks back to the stallion.

The stud still stands there, as though waiting for Frank to say something – words that will transcend their language barrier because of the truth in them. Words that will carry on the prairie winds and live forever.

Frank decides – his heart decides, not his head – that these horses he and his brother have come for today don't need to be part of a breeding program to make a better racehorse. These horses need to be saved because of exactly what they are.

That is what Frank Kuntz aims to do.

He searches within himself and finds the two words he will speak. Electricity hums through his body with the commitment he knows he's choosing. The truth of these words allows the prairie wind to lift them up and soar across the space between Frank and this stallion – the midnight stallion who almost crashed a helicopter and won his freedom.

"I promise."

* * *

Frank and Leo check out the pens all the horses have been brought to at the Dickinson public auction. The horses are segregated by sex and most of the foals are separated from their mothers. That is how they will be sold, in lots by age and sex.

Both Frank and Leo are surprised, really, to see how many survived the transportation process, especially since the cowboys at the round-up had run as many horses as they could into each stock trailer foals and all. Even that old gray mare and her baby made it, another testament to these horses' strength.

All the horses are tired, beat up, physically and mentally scarred, and shrunken. Most refuse to eat and hardly drink any water. They don't know what hay even is, much less a bucket.

Leo murmurs to Frank, "It's a lot quieter in here than I thought it would be."

"Of course it is," says Frank. "These horses have been demoralized, physically and mentally."

Leo shifts uneasily. "Those guys at the round-up have zero idea of the sensitivity level of these animals."

Frank says, "I think they get their jollies off o' picking on 'em."

Leo slaps Frank's arm and points to the stout blue roan stud. "Look at that big guy there. He's the one that fought so hard. Kept trying to jump out of the corral."

Franks sees the horse. He sees him all too clearly. "He's still covered in sweat and blood."

Leo pauses and thrums his suspenders nervously. "He should come home with us."

Frank just looks at his brother. "All of them should, Leo."

In another pen, they see the old gray mare and her foal with one white sock. She looks barely alive. Frank recalls some cowboys poking at her, once they finally caught her at the round-up, then laughing when she stumbled and crumpled to the dirt, only to get up again and rush to her baby.

Leo sets his jaw and just stares at the mare. He remembers the scene too. Frank can see his brother is going somewhere else in his mind right now –

someplace dark and terrible – so he stands by his side and shakes his head at it all.

Finally, Leo says, "It ain't right. How that round-up went." He stalks away toward the stands.

The brothers climb the bleachers, sit, and wait. Their bidding number sits hot in Leo's hand. Frank rubs his sweaty palms on his jeans as his leg bounces incessantly. They are both itching to get as many of these horses as possible home to safety.

The auctioneer's harsh, rhythmic song starts to echo around the metal building as the lots of four or five horses at a time are brought in, purchased, and ushered out. Leo bids on every strong and healthy-looking horse he can. All Frank has to do is keep nodding when his brother gives him a questioning glance. Their headcount is racking up quickly. At a penny over the kill barn bids, they can afford to keep going. So they do.

Eventually, the gray mare comes out with her foal. The little black colt is spry and feisty as ever. The mare looks beaten, exhausted, and traumatized more than her aged body can handle. Frank looks at Leo with a definite nod. Leo doesn't even hesitate. He sticks their number in the air, high, and the mare and foal are theirs for $25.00.

The brothers feel compelled to go see that the mother and foal get back into the pens securely, but before they even reach the gates, the mare spooks at the guys trying to get her to keep going. Like she knows this is her last chance to save her baby, she flings herself here and then there, but the men keep the pressure on from the rear. Then, in one horrible display of communication, the gate man and the rear prodder move at the exact same, bone-crushing time. The gate comes down with full force on the gray mare's head, wrenching her neck in an unnatural direction. She collapses, lifeless, to the ground.

Frank and Leo crash through the people in their way, yelling obscenities they save only for the worst of times. The shock of it rips through Frank like a razor. Leo looks like he's shifting into a combat mentality.

Saving that baby means everything to them in this moment. Frank knows he will allow the heartbreak of the mare to surge through him at another time – a time, most likely, when he is alone with a glass of whiskey – but now that baby is his priority.

The baby gets through the gates, through the alleys, and into the pens without trouble. Frank watches his movement as he follows him to the holding pens. His action is strong, and he carries himself, already at no more than three or four months old, with a distinguished, proud gate. Frank is beyond impressed with this little one.

The baby prances nervously around, searching for his mother. He's never been so far away from his mother. He zips from one side to the other quick and agile as a fox. Frank leans against the rail with a softness he's witnessed mares do hundreds of times with their foals.

Finally, the colt settles to a stop and stands as far away from Frank as the space will allow. He turns his head and looks at the man watching him. The foal's eyes glisten at Frank with a sadness he has witnessed before in moments of deep loss. They look at each other for a long while. Neither one expects anything from the other. Frank's heart goes out to him.

Then, the motherless foal inhales deeply and lets out his breath with a shaky flutter.

Frank says, "You're coming home with us, little Black Fox. And you will be safe."

Satisfied the colt is secure, Frank finds Leo, who is cussing out one of the men responsible for killing the mare. He pulls his brother off once he knows his point has been made. Together, emotionally stunned, they return to the stands.

As soon as they sit down, in comes a group with the stout blue roan in it, the big one that fought so hard to get free. Rank as ever. His fight with the world will never end.

He says, "The big one here is clearly the dominant one of the bunch."

Leo says, "We want that stud."

So Leo bids as usual, expecting it to go like the rest of them have while bidding against the kill buyers, but this time someone else starts bidding against him. Leo gives Frank a quizzical look, and Frank looks around. It takes no time at all to see that their competition is a young lady sitting alone in an empty section of the stands. If he's not mistaken, she seems an awful lot like the lady with the video camera at the round-up. He points her out to Leo, and the two keep bidding this lot of horses up and up.

Finally, Leo waves his hands to stop the auctioneer then hollers to him, "How many does she want?" They're not here to pay top dollar for these horses, no matter how impressive they are.

The auctioneer speaks into his microphone, his voice echoing like God around the building, "Ma'am, how many do you want?"

Without hesitation, she straightens her shoulders, holds up a finger, and says, "One."

Frank notices an inkling of uncertainty hidden within her confidence. She stares, unwavering, at the auctioneer and then at Frank and Leo with real nerve.

Frank evaluates her, as he assumes she's doing with them, right back. She's young, probably fresh out of college. She's nothing like some of the tough horsewomen he knows, especially the ones in his own family.

Quietly, he says to Leo, "I doubt she's after the big guy. I mean, *look* at her."

So Leo agrees, "Yep. No way she wants the big one." He nods to the auctioneer.

The auctioneer asks her, "Ma'am. What's your pick?"

"I want the big one."

* * *

Leo's voice carries firmly down the back alleys where they keep the horses. "You mind telling me just exactly what you think you're gonna do with that stud?"

The lady bidder stands outside her horse's pen. She snaps her head toward the brothers walking toward her, and Frank can tell by the death glare she's shooting them that she thinks they're kill-buyers coming for her horse. "None of your business," she snarls and turns her back on them.

Frank sees in her eyes, aside from the obvious defensiveness and anger, undertones of fear and a hint of desperation. She really does *not* know what she's going to do with this stud, this rank, angry, and wild stallion.

He can see Leo bristle at her attitude, so he steps in. "We're not kill-buyers, just so you know."

"Oh *really*? I've been watching you buy over 50 horses in there today." She sets her jaw, crosses her arms, and mimics Leo's voice. "You mind telling *me* just exactly what you think *you're* gonna do with that many wild horses?" Unruly bangs flop over one of her eyes making her look a little bedraggled, but she swoops her hair back, straightens her posture, and waits for an answer.

Leo, exhibiting mild restraint, says, "We *happen* to be taking them home."

She squints at him, not believing a word coming out of his mouth. She scoffs, "Ya right. Taking them *home*, huh?"

Frank raises his hands and softly pats the air to settle her down. "It's the truth." He places a hand on his chest. "I'm Frank Kuntz and this is my brother Leo. And we are not here to send these horses to the can. We're trying to save them. As many as possible."

Her scowl shifts from disgust to cautious curiosity.

Frank takes that as a softening, so he keeps going. "We ... we're impressed with these horses. They're amazing athletes. And, well, you saw at the round-up."

Her eyes widen slightly and she tips her head. She perhaps didn't think he'd seen her there.

"That was you," she says. "I saw you watching that little black stallion escape and nearly crash the helicopter."

Frank wonders if she had noticed how he had kept watching as that stallion fled for freedom. Did she witness his promise?

"I was there," he says. "and I hope you take that footage you got to the news too."

"It was the park's camera. I'll probably never see that footage. But I did take some pictures with my personal camera. I just might take those to the media. People need to know about that debacle."

When he sees her shoulders ease, he figures she's willing to hear more of what he has to say. "These animals got no stop in them. And my brother and I, we ride the cross-country races. We want to breed these horses with our racers. You know, make 'em stronger, hardier." He points to the stud's feet, "I mean, look at those feet! Like boulders."

Even Leo must be able to tell she's listening more openly now, because he pipes in, "exactly. And just look at his structure. That animal has got his feet under him, you know what I mean? Like, I've spent a lot of time watching them at the park, and let me tell you, these horses know where their feet are, no matter the terrain. They're good sons-a-bitches." He cuts himself off, hoping she doesn't shirk at his language.

One of her eyebrows shoots up as she continues to assess whether they are to be trusted. She turns to lean on the pen and watch her horse. The muscles in her jaw move, and she presses her lips together. Then she sets her forehead on the rail.

Her voice suddenly loses any pretense of confidence. It is small and quavering now. "I saw an injured mare in the barn get scooped up with a front-loader and dumped onto a trash pile today." She is visibly shaky but holds in her tears. "I don't understand this ugly world." Still staring into the stout blue's pen, she sighs softly and says, "Nocona."

Leo shoots Frank a confused look. Frank sort of shrugs. They both wait for her to say more.

They all watch the horse as a long silence lingers among them. The stallion's breathing is slow, and his coat is dry enough to see now that he is a blue roan, not black.

"That's his name. Nocona," she says finally. Then, with a deep sadness in her voice, "I named him after the last free war chief of the Comanche. The way he fought against those men, he should be free."

Frank can't even try to explain why humans behave the way they do, especially toward these horses. All he knows is that this horse belongs in their herd, not the park anymore. If he can keep her talking with them, they might have a chance at reasoning with her. "I, uh, noticed you didn't seem to be bidding on any other horses here at the auction." He lets his unasked question linger in the air.

She takes a deep, conceding breath and confesses what her plan actually had been. "I was going to set him free."

The brothers silently look at each other and then back at her.

"I couldn't stand the horrors. The round-up ... that ... it changed my ... I just don't understand how people can be so cruel. How inhumane *humans* choose to be! I couldn't just stand by and watch. I had to *do something*. So I got in my car, drove to the nearest phone, which was a half hour away in Minot, and called the Humane Society. when they said they couldn't do anything, I drove all the way back. All I kept thinking about on that drive back was how I had to do something for him. I knew I couldn't do anything for the whole herd," she laughs, "I mean, look at me. I'm new to the area, I know hardly anyone. I just had it in my mind that if I could at least save *him* ..." She exhales, and her whole demeanor sags. "I don't know." She looks at the brothers and says it again. "I don't know. I just knew I had to save *this horse*. This *one horse* right here."

Leo gives a little scoff, but Frank steps in quickly with a mild, understanding tone, "Okay. It sounds like we've all got the same idea in mind here." He nods to her. "That's good. That's a start.

"Can I ask you your name?" He extends a hand.

She eyes him somewhat sheepishly and extends her hand too. "Castle. Castle McLaughlin."

Frank smiles and takes her hand warmly. "It's nice to meet you, Castle."

* * *

Sitting at a picnic table outside the stands, Frank, Leo, and Castle McLaughlin sip at their coffee from the concessions. Little curls of steam rise from the Styrofoam cups as they get to talking. Before too long, they are visiting like old friends.

Chuckling, Leo says, "So let me see if I got this straight. You borrowed your neighbor's two-horse trailer, hornswoggled a vet into giving you some sedative and a syringe, got some park service lackey to give you a key to the back gate, so you could transport that stallion back to the park, and then just let him loose."

Castle nearly spits out her coffee as she laughs at the obvious ridiculousness of it all. "That's about it. I figured the park doesn't know one horse from another. Which they don't. They'd never know what happened."

Frank can't help but smile at this lady's naivety, but he is glad they're all sitting down and talking. Her passion for the horses is real.

She shakes her head at herself. "I'd been standing by his pen before you guys got there, watching this larger-than-life, wild stallion which I can't even touch, much less get close enough to sedate him! I'm wondering how the heck am I going to do this? I mean, here's this eleven-hundred-pound stud – he's never going to fit in a 2-horse trailer, even if I could get him in there." She looks around and says quietly, "and no way, no how was I going to ask any of these horrible men to help me."

They all chuckle and shake their heads. The ice has broken.

Leo asks, "So you're new to the area. What brought you all the way out here?"

She takes a sip and then freely explains. "I moved here a month ago to work for the National Park Service. I'm a grad student, and I've been working for the Knife River Indian Villages National Historic Site in Stanton as an interpretive ranger. See, I'm an anthropologist and a lifelong horsewoman, so my park sent me here. I was hired to work on the round-up and learn about the horses."

Both Frank's and Leo's eyebrows pop up at this little surprise.

She goes on, "Mhm. I was supposed to ride in that round-up." Her eyes flit to Leo then away. "Thank God I didn't."

Frank figures she knew Leo was riding that day.

Leo says sincerely and solemnly, "ya. That was a bad one, I'd say."

She eh-hems and continues. "They ended up giving me a camera instead. I couldn't get any answers to any of my questions about the horses and their history. So they invited me to write a grant proposal to do research. They're going to fund me. I assume they'll assign me to some key people for the project. Maybe you guys."

Frank nods and gestures to his brother. "Leo here has done a lot, and I mean a lot, of research already."

"Oh?" she says.

Leo nods too. "Yep. I'll get you pointed in the right direction, that's a for sure."

Frank adds, "You know, that stud, Nocona you're calling him, he can come to our place." He raises his hands, "He's *your* horse, no two ways about that, but he can be a part of something pretty neat if you let him contribute to our breeding program. Plus, he'll be with a lot of his own herd there. It'll be better than sending him back to the park where they'll just keep rounding him up again and again."

Castle looks hesitant yet optimistic. "You think? I'm going to want to come see him."

"Absolutely," Leo pipes in. "You're gonna need to come and get your history lessons from me anyway." He offers a small smile and a rare wink.

Castle smiles back and says, "Okay then. I'll send him home with you."

Relief washes over Frank. He also feels proud of this brave, naïve, and passionate young woman.

He says, "If we can work together, we can make it work."

* * *

Only one foal is born the next year. The mares all aborted after the round-up.

* * *

Photo Gallery Index

1. Leo Kuntz Family
2. Frank and Christa assess the new situation after bringing the horses home.
3. Frank Kuntz in his military uniform
4. Frank Kuntz Farm - early years
5. Frank with grandsons Beckett and Frankie, and part of their Nokota herd. (Photo by Nikki Doll)
6. Frank, Charlie and Leo
7. Frank – Cross-country Race MC 1986 (Photo by Castle McLaughlin)
8. Frank – Cross-country Race MC 1989 (Photo by Castle McLaughlin)
9. Medora von Hoffman, the Marquise de Mores, posing as the quintessential frontier lady. Courtesy State Historical Society of North Dakota 0042-81.
10. Leo (Frank's Father) and Pauline (Frank's Mother) Kuntz
11. Nocona, a dominant Ranch type herd stallion being removed from the park, 1986. Photo by Castle McLaughlin.
12. Frank and Leo's first horse sale flyer
13. Frank and his daughters Dawn, Alecia, and Christa
14. Frank talking with Red Eagle's person. 2020. (Photo by Cher Renky Van Hoecke
15. Frank and Muddy in Pennsylvania 2023 (Photo taken from Facebook video posted by Kuntz Nokota Ranch)
16. Finale! Photo courtesy of The Nokota Challenge

Photo Gallery – Page 1

LEO KUNTZ FAMILY
Patty, Bob, Ed, Leo, Frank, David, Wendelin, Connie, Felicia, Karleen, Pauline, Leo, Jerry, Joe

Photo Gallery – Page 2

FRANK KUNTZ FAMILY
Dawn, Alicia, Krista, Frank

Chapter 13
Letting Go, Moving On

Sometimes letting things go is an act of far greater power than hanging on.
~ Eckhart Tolle

2023

"I won't make them go through another winter like last year," Frank says to Shelly. "I just can't. I won't."

She breathes deeply for him and nods in agreement, slow and calm. Then she says, "Okay. We've got that established. The horses will not endure another winter like last year." She gives a definitive nod. "It's good we've got a few of our older mares going to good retirement homes. That's a good thing. One to Minnesota and the other two to Kentucky. Their new people are going to spoil them so much."

Frank softens into a genuine grin. "God, that's the truth. We're so fortunate to have found those folks. The old girls deserve the best life they can give 'em." Even though it is so hard to see any of his horses go, knowing how good they're going to have it compared to here right now makes it an easy decision to let them go."

"I'm looking forward to a road trip," Shelly says. "What other ideas have you got up your sleeve, Frank? What about the lot you said were going to go to Standing Rock? When we went to the Greasy Grass races there in June, didn't a few people say they were interested in buying a bunch of horses from us?"

He pops several colorful pills of various shapes and sizes, then drains his coffee cup. He shoves back from the table and goes to the entry to get his boots. "They had mentioned how they would like to have horses from their own history in their pastures." He sighs and shakes his head. "I haven't heard much from them. But that's okay. They'll let me know when they're ready."

Shelly takes his emptied pill organizer back to its spot on the counter next to hers and starts unscrewing caps from several prescription bottles to start filling up another week's worth for both of them. She says, "It's a lot to take on several horses. Even if they are free. I get it."

His eyes are set in that way they always get when he's chewing hard on an idea. All he says as he smashes his hat down is, "I'm working on something with that outfitter ranch in Montana."

"Oh? They're still interested?"

He nods. "They are. Haven't said when, but they want all the pony-crosses. Those horses will make good trail mounts and broodmares."

A short silence hangs between them. He and his wife discussed it at length. Letting their pony-crosses go – the progeny of Kuntz ponies like good old Sundance and Chico – feels like cutting down a huge branch of their family tree and letting it get washed down the river. They will probably never see any of them again, the flaxen manes and tails, the butterscotch coats that glisten in the sun like gold, and those mischievous but soft, brown eyes peeking from behind long, fluffy forelocks. Several, he had hoped, would be for his grandsons. Christa has already started working with a couple even. It was no surprise how quickly those ponies took to the little boys.

The outfitter Frank is talking about, however, will be a good home for them. They will be cared for and loved. Many will be broodmares, so their line will live on, just not with the Kuntz family anymore.

Shelly offers, "I'm glad they're going together. They'll have each other." The last words catch a little in her throat, but she manages a strong smile for her husband.

She changes the subject and asks, "Are you still planning to go speak for Chasing Horses? I know how nervous you get when you have to speak in front of a big crowd, but you did so great at their rally this summer."

It's true, ever since he was just a high schooler when he had to take that godforsaken speech class, he's hated public speaking. He gets so nervous and shaky. His palms get all clammy and somehow his mouth becomes incapable of generating saliva. When he starts advocating for the Nokota horses, though, all that nervousness melts away. His passion for doing what is right for them takes over in the form of knowledge, experience, and love.

He nods. "I'll do whatever I can to help them out. That herd needs help too. I'm not a fan of their *birth control* methods. We need to support each other however we can."

Shelly agrees, "Mmhm. At least they've stopped those horrible helicopter round-ups. It's really great how they're willing to provide a tax-exempt charity link through their organization for everyone wanting to help *our* horses exclusively." She sort of chuckles. "Did you ever imagine that you would one day be advocating for the same horses you fought the park about back in the round-up days? The ones they insisted on developing by introducing domestic breeds into the park in order to change the geno/phenotype of the Nokota? It's funny how things change." She butters a piece of toast and hands it to him. "Here, you need to eat after taking those pills, remember."

"I know," he says obediently, then chews and says, "think how I've fought to have the park slowly introduce the Nokota back into their herd too. I don't think there will ever be horses in that park without drama of some kind."

Shelly butters her own piece of toast, nodding and mmhmming. "It's interesting to see how that herd has changed over the last 30 years too."

His eyes brighten at that. "Exactly. Now they're starting to look like Nokotas. They're showing a square build, full neck, and blue roan colors. The strongest strains are coming back." Then his eyes scowl again. "But that's not where our herd belongs either. Jeez, I don't even know if getting Standing Rock to take them in is the right thing. Of course, our mission is and always will be to get them back to their people, but the people have to want them back too. Even my friends over there aren't sure they are ready to take them back. Nope. Our horses need a private place of their own unencumbered by politics – state, federal, or tribal. A place where we can all meet together and help each other carry out the Nokota legacy."

Shelly can hear the frustration building in his voice, so she tries changing the subject. "Aren't the few babies we got this year just the most darling you've ever seen?"

Frank can't argue that. "Yep. Lots of color from Coyote. He's a good stud. I'm not worried about the lethal white gene as much as everyone else seems to be. You know, back when Leo and I first started this whole breeding program, we didn't know anything about that kind of stuff. We just let nature take its course like it would in the wild. But that's when we had the space to let the horses be horses."

"And fewer people telling you how *they* think you should do things."

Shelly lets that sit for a moment. Lethal white is an incredibly sad condition to watch a foal die from. They are born all white with blue eyes, and their intestines don't fully develop so they can't process nourishment. Some breeding experts say any horse with color, like a paint or a blue roan, can carry the gene for it. Many of his best horses – Nocona, Painted Lady, Papa Smoke – were paints or roans. Coyote is a blue roan, but so far, the babies have been fine. She knows how painful it is for her husband to see any of their horses cross over into the spirit world, much less a baby. She knows how it wrecks him emotionally when he has to, God forbid, put one down.

He says soberly, "I don't think we'll have many, if any, babies next year. I can't give 'em the environment I want. But at least we have the rental pasture for some of the mares this summer. When people say they want to come see the horses, I don't want them to have to see the yard."

This happens on occasion. Someone learns about Frank and the Nokota and come to visit the horses. It's happened several times this summer, and he genuinely enjoys having new and old followers visit. It's always a rewarding experience watching people fall in love with the breed just by spending time in their presence. His horses are pretty magical that way.

Shelly recites his common line, "We'll do the best we can with the tools we've got."

Frank nods and forces a smile for his beautiful wife, always by his side, forever in his corner.

She starts to organize some papers that have been piling up at the kitchen table. "Remember, we've got our little camping trip to the river with the kids this weekend. Got your fishing things ready?"

"I'm looking forward to that. And I will."

"Good. I'm sure the boys are too."

"Well," Frank says, getting up from the table, "I better get motivated here and go get that hay up."

"You get the tractor working again?"

"The part came a couple days ago. We'll see if it holds up. The mower's what I'm worried about now. Making a funny noise. I'll have to take a look at that."

Shelly smiles and shakes her head, "Always something, isn't it, hun."

He opens the door to leave for the farm and looks out into the misty morning. "Always something."

Chapter 14
Transition

The journey in between what you once were and who you are now becoming is where the dance of life takes place.
~ Barbara De Angelis

1986 Continued

Rolling up his driveway after that long, emotionally draining day at the auction, Frank feels like something is wrong. It's not something he can see, per se, but something he feels. An air of emptiness cascades over the farm and little house.

When he shuts off the truck, his hand lingers on the key in the ignition as he looks around. The house is so still. So quiet.

He opens the front door and hollers his typical, "I'm home! Where are my girls?" His mouth hangs open at the sight of an empty room, and not just empty of people, but of furniture, decorations, and things that make it a home.

She has left him. Maria has decided. This life is not what she signed up for. She is gone.

Although there had been many signs, Frank had chosen not to see them. The time away from home, the business of life, the horses, and the different visions for their future, all created blinders while they grew apart.

Maria will ask for a divorce. He will say he doesn't want to get divorced. A good German Catholic boy, no matter how young and naïve, takes care of his family. That's how he was raised. She will insist, and in time, he will realize it was for the best.

He will gain full custody of the girls as Maria goes back to California. Eventually, he will make sure his daughters keep in touch with their mother through phone calls, letters, and maybe a visit at some point.

Frank and his beautiful children will find their new normal together.

* * *

1988

It's been a couple of years since Frank and Leo brought the herd home. Between both his dad's place and his own, these horses consume most of Frank's time.

Their breeding program is going just fine. He's particularly excited about the pony crosses they're getting from his dad's driving ponies and the park horses. In truth, so far, any cross with a park horse has turned out to be a hardy, intelligent, compassionate addition. The park horses' bloodlines are strong.

"Daaaad," hollers five-year-old Christa, "these buckets are too heavy! I can't do it." She drops the two five-gallon buckets that are almost as tall as she is and stomps her tiny foot, making the pigtails on top of her head boing around like antennae.

Myloose, the calico cat, winds around her legs, purring and sniffing inside each bucket, but she can't console little Christa this time. A butterfly flits around the cat's head, so she takes a swipe and bounces after it. Summertime is in full swing, complete with bugs and humidity.

It's feeding time for the hard keepers and older mares of their herd that stay up by the barn. Frank, carrying grain buckets to them, turns around and goes to his youngest daughter.

He squats down and lifts her pouting chin. "I can take the water buckets, Hunny. You can take this grain bucket."

She doesn't look happy about that either and thumps her fists on her hips to say, "I don't want to carry the grain bucket."

"Well then, what *do* you want?" he asks her.

She scrunches her face. "I want to be *strong enough* to carry the water."

Frank takes a moment to digest this. Christa could be inside playing with her toys, but here she is doing chores with her daddy. She wants to show him how strong she is. He knows he should carry the water buckets for her, but that is not what he decides to do. Instead, he says, "Let's just remember that these horses have us, and that's it. They can't get their water by themselves. They're counting on us to take care of them. To keep them around forever."

Christa looks down at her shoes. Then, with a face so serious it makes Frank's eyebrows go up, she shoves up imaginary sleeves, grabs both handles of the water buckets, and bears down deep with a red-faced grimace. Somehow, Christa finds the strength within to carry those splashing water buckets all the way to the pen.

It takes great restraint for Frank not to help her as she struggles. His greatest instinct is to protect his children, but he knows this is what she wants. She wants to show her strength. So, he lets her.

Christa lets the buckets fall hard onto the ground and says, "See, Dad. I can do it. You didn't think I could, but I did it."

"Yes, you did," he says with pride which seems to satisfy her.

While the horses drink and eat grain, father and daughter lean on the fence and watch. The sound of content chewing and tail swishing plays a rhythm in the humid air. They hear music playing in the house. Alecia must be making one of her famous mixed tapes from the radio again.

Eventually, he says, "You know, I see how strong you are. I see you get stronger every day. But you're my little girl, and if anything ever happened to you, well, I would never forgive myself. Does that make sense?"

Christa looks up at him with her deep dark eyes and says, "I guess so. But you're right, I'm super strong." She folds her arm to make a muscle and points to her elbow.

Frank says seriously, "Oh that's for sure, you are."

Coming from the house, he hears Dawn and Alecia having one of their clashes. It's probably about the phone again. It's Friday, and they had both asked if they could go out with friends, so he knows his older daughters will get into scuffs over hairspray and clothes at some point too. Dawn and Alecia will work it out like they always do.

Christa pays no attention to the noises coming from the house. She starts to climb through the rails.

Frank catches her before she slips all the way through and says, "Hey, hey, whatcha doin'?"

"I'm gonna go pet them. They want me to pet them."

Frank notices the horses are done eating, standing quietly with low heads, and sort of gazing at her with gentle, soulful eyes. Those eyes, that look, it's different than with the domestic horses, even Charlie. There are words behind a wild one's gaze. He is learning every day what they say. These content mares with full bellies say they are ready for some affection.

"I think you're right. Let's go in together."

With her tiny hand in his, they go through the gate and stand still. He knows these horses are used to people now that they've been home for so long, but this is as perfect a teaching moment as ever.

He says, "Now, we need to listen to the horses."

Christa's eyes get big as she leans forward with one hand cupped to her ear. "They're not saying anything. I can't hear them."

"Aw, but that's where you're wrong. See, look at their ears. Look at their body. Now, we're going to approach them in a way that says we have no intentions, no expectations for them to do anything but just let us be in their presence. That's their gift to us."

Christa listens to his words and stands by his side. In a matter of minutes, one mare, then two, come close enough for her to reach and softly scratch. Frank sees the smile curl up the sides of her mouth, and he listens to her sweet voice say kind things to them. He gently brushes away the flies when they land. One mare closes her eyes and lets her bottom lip dangle. The other mare breathes deeply and lets out a blissful sigh, spraying Christa's shoulder a little.

Since the round-up and auction, Frank and Leo have known these horses need protecting. They were all frightened, full of flight and fight, but Frank promised they would be safe. Every day, he tries to create an atmosphere for them – whether out in the pastures or here in a pen – that reminds them they don't have to run anymore. The two-leggeds are here to help soothe the hurts of their past and create a future full of beauty and life and love.

In his heart of hearts, he knows these animals could make a mark in the horse world if people just learn about them and get to know them. There's nothing these athletes can't do. It's just a matter of earning their trust and respect to teach them what you're asking them to do. Ultimately, however, Frank believes the best thing he and his brother can strive for is to find a permanent home for a large herd of these ponies, back with their people, the Hunkpapa Lakota, somehow, someday. That is where they belong.

Frank says to his daughter, "These horses are here with us now. Like Uncle Leo says, we need to make friends with them. We will feed them, water them, pet them. We must be kind and love each one. But don't fall *in love* with them because one day, they will be returned to their people and to the plains that once were theirs. I've made a promise to do that for them. Does that make sense?"

Christa nods solemnly as she continues to rub the silky coat and says, with wisdom beyond her years, "I promise too."

* * *

1989

Leo comes barging through the front door, lets the screen door slam, and plops right down at Frank's kitchen table. He leans back, props his feet up, and crosses his arms. "Well, she did it."

Frank turns from the stove where he is cooking his morning eggs. He raises an eyebrow at his brother, which prompts Leo to take his feet off the table. "Good morning to you too," he says with a sideways grin. "Eggs?"

"Yah, I'd take some if you got 'em."

Frank opens his fridge to get more eggs. He blocks Leo's view, not wanting him to see its painfully sparse contents. "Who did what?" he asks.

"Castle," Leo replies. "Our girl Castle finished her report. I just got the call this morning. It's officially available through the National Park Service." He sweeps his hands through the air like reading a headline. *"The History and Status of the Wild Horses of Theodore Roosevelt National Park."* He makes his voice sound like a TV announcer and says, "Request your copy today!"

Frank takes one of the girls' breakfast plates from the sink and quickly washes it up for him. "She did, did she? I'll be damned. How many pages did it turn out to be?"

"Over 500!" Leo exclaims.

Frank cracks the last of the fresh eggs the girls had gathered before they got on the school bus this morning. It sizzles and pops in the hot pan.

This report Castle has been working on since they met her a few years ago is really something. He and Leo are so amazed at how crazy smart this gal is – so educated, so capable of great things. She'd shown him several drafts as it progressed – side notes, scribblings, paragraphs crossed out. Leo and Tom Tescher, one of the ranchers the Park hires for round-ups, had been her official advisors. Frank contributed too. It was all there. All the history behind the horses. Documentation that they are descendants of Sitting Bull's war ponies. Fact after fact laid out in plain English for the world to read and learn. He feels fortunate to have met Castle and, in a sense, have her in their corner when it comes to the horses.

Castle's horse Nocona has made a big impact in their breeding program. With all the time she has spent visiting that big brute, she has been around enough to feel like part of the family. She has experienced many-a Kuntz family meal with several of them crowded at the table, scrapping for food, and razzing each other. She's heroized his mother Pauline for putting up with all of them and being able to cook three squares for such a rowdy lot.

Now that her report is done, Frank imagines they will be seeing a bit less of her, but she has, like he and Leo, fallen in love with the park horses. It's not just on a fascination or curiosity level either but on a personal investment level.

"This is huge, don't ya know," says Leo as he sits forward to eat his eggs. "I mean, people really oughta know about these horses. If they learn how good these animals are at any job they're asked to do," his eyes are big and his face is lit up. "my god, people are gonna want to buy them."

Leo has been putting a lot of time into training the park horses. Leo doesn't do things quite like Frank, but he admires what a true horseman his brother is and always has been. Leo likes to get things done quickly. They both learned right away that you have to get all the cowboy out of you when you start working with one of the park horses.

The bit of training Frank has been able to squeeze into his days has shown him, hands down, how true Leo's words are.

Frank agrees, "They're smart, all right. It's all about eye contact and body language. Once you get their trust, seems there's nothing they won't do for you. It's definitely different than with our domestic horses. Absolutely. If we can get them out into the right hands, these horses will sell themselves."

Leo jabs a finger at Frank, "Exactly! Oh, that reminds me. I need to borrow your fencing pliers and crimping tools. The big bastard Nocona took down a line on the north end." He ruefully chuckles, "Let's just say he's not a fan of the four-wheeler."

Frank nods with understanding. He knows very well that you can't push the wild ones too hard when getting them from one pasture to another. They'll simply say, "I'm outta here," and plow through whatever.

He answers, "Yep, they're in the shed on the bench in a bucket. Just put 'em back when you're done." He knows he might have to go get them back himself. Leo can be forgetful sometimes.

"Anyway," Leo continues, "that's why I think we need to organize a sale. We gotta get these horses to ranchers. Can you manage that?"

Frank takes the plate from the table and turns to wash it in the sink. He likes this idea of a sale. They need people to see what "doing" horses these are. If they need to help people know more about them, the horses will create a reputation for themselves. This could be the next step toward finding a permanent home for a core herd and getting them back with their people.

He glances at an unopened envelope on the counter. It's another notice from the bank about the house. Interest rates have soared in the last few years. He's barely hanging onto it. It nearly broke his heart last night when Christa told him she needed money for a school field trip. He'd dug into his pockets and pulled out all he had – a dollar bill and a handful of change. She had given him that beyond-her-years protective look she's had since she was two. Then, something shifted in her and she said, just as innocent and cheery as ever, "Oh, I forgot. The school is going to pay for everything." Then she bounded away to her room.

Yes, selling some horses would be a good thing.

"Frank, can you manage that?" Leo breaks into Frank's thoughts.

Frank bobs his head, slowly at first, then with more fervor. "I can absolutely manage that." His wheels started turning. "We need a name."

"You want to go with the idea I've been tossing around?"

Frank says, "The words North and Dakota merged?"

"That's it. Nokota," Leo says, his eyes sort of starry at the thought. "After the land they came from and the land they belong to."

"It's a good name," Frank agrees as he thinks, *And the land they're going back to.* "

The brothers look at each other for a moment, sealing the agreement with their eyes.

Frank moves on with the logistics racing through his head. "Can't sell a horse without a brand transfer. I know you've had your head set on using the Huidekoper brand from that historical HT Ranch, and I get it, that ranch played a huge part in these horses' history, but that's a Z4. The Stockman's Association says you can't use numbers anymore. How you gonna get that approved?"

Leo gives the wiliest look and says, "I got that figured out, brother. I already submitted it. Told them it's an LT. I'm just inverting the L."

Impressed with the clever idea, Frank smiles. "Well, I guess we got it all figured out then, don't we?"

Leo leans forward toward the window. "Hey. Does Myloose want in?"

Frank looks and sees their calico cat at the window begging to come in like a dog. "I suppose so," he says, shaking his head and going to the door to let her inside.

Leo grins at the scene. "Where's that black tomcat you had coming around here?"

Frank thinks for a second, "You mean Ralph?"

"Yah! That's it. Ralph. I figured we'd be seeing a whole boatload of kittens pretty soon."

Frank picks up Myloose and tries to pet her, but she gives a curt little squawk, scrambles out of his arms, and trots off to one of the girls' rooms.

"Nope. He didn't want to stick around. Too many women in the house!"

* * *

Frank is out in the garden, weeding and picking cucumbers and other vegetables for the girls' after-school snack when the school bus stops at the end of the driveway. Dawn and Alecia climb down and head for the house like they do every day, but Christa, all glum-faced drags her feet straight to the barn.

Something's up. Instead of tracking her down right away, he takes the vegetables to the kitchen sink and starts to wash them.

He can hear loud music playing in Alecia's room. He knows she'll get her homework done. She always does. That is one kid who he doesn't have to worry about getting good grades. It's always driven her sister nuts how she barely studies and still gets straight As and Bs.

Dawn comes into the kitchen with a stack of books and papers. He's proud of how seriously she takes her schoolwork. It's a good thing she tends to get to it right away since it doesn't come as quickly as she wishes some days. Dawn sets her stack down on the table with a thud and goes to check the fridge.

He asks her, "Something wrong with your littlest sister? She went straight to the barn without so much as a hello."

Giving up on the contents of the fridge, Dawn gets a glass of water. She grabs a peeler and starts helping Frank. "I'm not totally sure, but I think some boys at the back of the bus were teasing her about something," she offers. "I tried asking her what was wrong, but she didn't want to talk about it. I'll tell Alecia to go see if she'll talk to her."

She starts to go, but Frank stops her.

He wipes his hands on a dish towel and says, "I'll go to her. You get a start on your homework."

Their dog Blue gets up off the front step to follow him as he sets off across the yard. Halfway to the barn, he can already see Christa's silhouette sitting on a haybale outside her little Appaloosa's stall. She is petting Myloose curled up on her lap.

Blue trots off into the corners of the barn looking for critters. Frank leans in the doorway and puts his hands in his pockets. "Nothing like a good horse to tell your troubles to."

Christa looks up but doesn't reply. He sees her tears but doesn't make a big thing about it. Instead, he strolls to the stall and scratches the pony's ears.

"How's Sparkles doing today?"

The speckled Appaloosa's eyes roll up as he leans hard into Frank's hand.

Christa's voice comes out small, "He's itchy."

Frank chuckles softly, "I see that." Then he finishes his scratching, and Sparkles shakes his head in pure delight, thankful for the relief. "Mind if I join you on your haybale there?"

She slides over to the edge, making room for him.

"You seem a little down in the dumps. Want to tell me about it?"

At first, she says nothing, and for Frank, that is okay. He waits and waits while they listen to Sparkles munch on hay and the birds in the loft twitter and flutter.

Finally, he hears her say, "The kids at the back of the bus call me names."

Internally he wants to know who it was and what names they called her *right now*, but he doesn't say anything. He gives her time to go on.

"They make fun of my skin. Because it's so dark. They said I'm not allowed to touch anything." She looks up at him with a painful, confused expression. "Why, Dad? Why can't I touch anything just because my skin is dark? Am I that different than everyone else?"

It takes a moment for him to find the words he wants her to hear – the words he wants her to remember for the rest of her life. He says, "Well, they aren't making fun of you because you're different. Those kids are just jealous of your beautiful skin and your beautiful face." He looks her in the eye. "Never, never let anyone tell you otherwise."

Christa gazes back at her dad. He can see she believes every word he says. He smiles and wipes a tear away with his rough thumb. To his great relief, his little girl smiles back at him.

"How about we saddle up Charlie and Sparkles here and take them out for a run?"

Her eyes light up along with the rest of her. She pops off the hay bale and grabs the halter hanging on a nail. "Yes!"

They go racing across the fields, letting the ugly parts of her day get swept away into the wind, never to be seen again.

Chapter 15
Land!

Where no one intrudes, many can live in harmony.
~ Chief Dan George

2023

"Dad!" Christa says as she jumps out of her car and rushes to Frank.

Immediately, Frank thinks something is wrong, but then he sees her tapping her phone. Her face is lit up like it's Christmas.

Before he even has a chance to say hello or put down the bucket of water he is hauling to the saddle horses, she is right by his side saying, "Look at this!"

She shoves the phone to his face, and he leans back to try to see it. It's probably some new merchandise she's designed and put on their website. She's so good at coming up with products that have their logo, and people like to buy the stuff. It's not a huge money-maker, although it does help pay for some daily needs for the horses'. It mostly gets their new logo and name out to their followers who have been asking how they can show their support. Still, so many people want to help save these horses with him.

He squints and says, "What is it?" He squints harder.

"It's land, Dad!" she practically squeals. "Land for the horses!"

He screws up his face and gives her a look of disbelief. "Come on. Let's go to the shed. I'm gonna need my cheaters for this."

She walks with him as she keeps scrolling looking at the real estate ad she has found.

"Where are the boys?" Frank asks. He thought she would bring them so they could help do chores. He always looks forward to watching the boys be with the horses.

"I left them with Grandma Shelly. You and I need to talk about this." She waves her phone at him.

When they get inside, he turns on a fan and sits at the little table where his cheaters are. He snaps them together at the bridge of his nose. "All right now, lemme see what you've got there."

Christa sets her phone on the table and looks over his shoulder as she taps and scrolls for him. "It's way over a thousand acres. It's perfect, Dad. There's a natural water source. Prairie and terrain like Nokotas know and love. It's enough space for the horses to form natural bands and live the way they are supposed to. It even has electricity available on site. We could build our sanctuary and interpretive center there. It's in a great location too. We could really draw in tourists. And the best part is," she sits to look him in the eye, "it would be ours. Private property. I was thinking, we could put together a family foundation to ensure that no one else can invade or try to take it away."

She stops abruptly to take a breath, and Frank can see the glossiness of her eyes. Her energy is catching as always. It makes a glimmer of excitement flicker inside himself.

She shakes off the threat of the tears on the brim and says, "Heck. You could have coffee with the ponies in your underwear whenever you want!"

That makes him laugh out loud. "It looks amazing, Christa. It really does." He scrolls through the pictures on the real estate website and can easily imagine his herd running free on this land. He dares to picture a simple setup for a sanctuary where people can come and learn about the Nokota. Maybe a small therapeutic facility for horses like Shelly's Bella. He even goes so far as to envision the interpretive center his family has talked about. They would create a space where the native people of North Dakota, like his friends at Standing Rock, could share their arts, crafts, and skills with others.

Then, he looks at the price.

His eyes just about bug out of his head. He lights up a cigarette and starts bouncing his leg. "The taxes alone will be near impossible to make happen."

Christa catches on quickly. "Oh. Don't worry about that."

"*Don't worry about that*?! We don't even know how we're going feed these guys."

She cuts in and keeps going, "It's fully fenced and has an established road running right through it. And look," she taps to the listing's description, "tons of tillable land and a percentage of mineral rights. If we do this right and get creative, the land could help support itself."

Frank shakes his head. But inside, he is still dreaming. It has been a while since he's felt excited about his family's future.

He blows out a long stream of smoke. "We need to talk to the family about this."

"Absolutely! I've already put a bug in Dawn's ear." She grabs her phone and starts texting. Giddy, she says, "I'll tell Dawn and Alecia. We need a family meeting." She walks away talking to herself listing other people she wants to notify.

He picks up his phone to call Shelly. They're all going to need a dose of some of her unflinching faith for this. Even if this whole thing is just a pipe dream, seeing his daughter so excited is worth giving it some attention. What can it hurt to hope on a dream?

Later that night, he sees Christa has updated their GoFundMe page:

"Help Grandpa Frank Save the Horses!"

"We found them land to call their forever home! ATTENTION!! Land to roam, without government control and BLM to use them as test subjects or to try one day to eradicate them again! A true place to call home!

We never thought we would find something that could be so perfect for the horses, not to mention a place where it would bring tourism and potential income to the tribe. A place where they could come together once again, the way it is meant to be!

URGENT – as the winter months are right around the corner, I know it is possible to give these horses their forever home to be protected for always!

We have updated our GoFundMe as well. Dreams do come true if you work hard enough for them."

The dollar amount in the upper corner says: *$4,000,000 goal.*

Of course, it seems impossible, but Frank is no stranger to "impossible" things happening in his life. He has learned that whenever his head says, *What are the chances?* the winds of fate have their way of delivering the biggest blessings.

Chapter 16
Love Story

I wanna love somebody, love somebody like you.
~ Keith Urban

1991 – September 12, 1992

Frank and Maria have been divorced for a long time now, but he continues to insist that his daughters stay in contact with her. He tells them that even though he is not married to their mom anymore, he is so glad that he and Maria had their time together. If it weren't for her, the best parts of his entire life wouldn't exist. He will forever be grateful for the beautiful children Maria brought into this world with him.

He embraces life as a single dad, but on occasion, he finds himself seeking that one person with whom he can share his life. Realistically, though, he knows he can't expect anyone to take on all that has become his life. What are the chances, anyway, that a guy like him – divorced father of three teenage daughters, hopelessly rapt in a rare breed of horse, and barely has a spare dime to his name – would be lucky enough to find a woman willing to embrace his world?

What are the chances?

* * *

It is the Fourth of July weekend, and the city of Minneapolis is humming and bustling. To most city-dwellers, the crazy-busy metropolitan life is what makes them feel alive. Traffic, buildings, and crowds of people typically ensure no one ever feels alone.

For one recently divorced young woman, however, as she paces around her little apartment, the city has never made her feel more alone. It's fine that her two daughters live with their dad most of the time. Thank God they're taking the separation as well as they are. She just misses them and the raucous activity they add to her day.

This stillness makes the apartment's walls close in. So much quiet makes her heart ache for home – Bismarck, North Dakota.

Even though she is young, healthy, and as vibrant as ever, Shelly Hauge is lonely.

She picks up the phone and tries to make her voice vibrant and bright as usual. "Hey Dad, what are you and Barb up to this weekend? Need a little company? I was thinking of maybe coming for a visit?"

Her dad's voice wraps around her like a warm blanket. He sounds so happy. "Shelly! My goodness, it's good to hear my little girl's voice. I was just thinking about you. We're heading to Medora for the weekend. Thought you should come along. Take a break from the big city life, eh? I'm bringing the horses. Gonna do some trail riding with the horse club. Whaddya say, Shell?"

A sigh of grateful relief gushes through her. After a moment, her emotions settle. "I would love to, Dad." She looks around her apartment and knows she can be out the door in minutes. "See you in a few hours."

He laughs a little at her immediate response. "We'll be here. The motorhome is ready to roll."

The six-hour drive flies by, as the road to home often does, and before she knows it, she is winding her way through the familiar streets and neighborhoods of Bismarck. When she pulls up to her folks' driveway, she slams it in park, and leaps out of her car to launch into her dad's open arms. She holds him tight, and though her lingering embrace surprises him a little, he lets her melt into him and hugs her back as long as she needs.

When she pulls away finally, he holds her at arm's length, looks at her with those sun-creased eyes, and says, "I'm glad you came."

Barb reaches in to give Shelly a welcoming hug too. She knows how good it feels to see your family after being away for some time. When she lets go, she says with a laugh, "Now toss your bag in the motorhome, and let's hit the road!"

"Do you want me to bring a horse along for you?" Shelly's dad asks.

Shelly thinks about it for a second. It's always fun riding with her folks, but this time she really, *really* just wants some serious R and R. There is no better place for that than beautiful Medora.

"I'll sit this one out, Dad."

"Suit yourself," he says and goes to load the horses.

In another swoosh of time, they are heading even further west into Badland territory. Elements of civilization start to peel away from the landscape, opening up to a vast world of prairie, buttes, and just so much *space*.

When they roll into the east side of Medora, they park the RV and horse trailer at the Rancherama campground. Pines and spruces perfume the air along with whisps of campfires. The "quiet" she has escaped from is replaced with relaxed snorts and murmurs of tied horses at trailers and high lines. Birds flit happily from camp to camp singing their cheery tunes over the day-to-day chatter of people going about their business. It creates a soothing soundtrack that envelops Shelly's soul. Any lingering tension in her muscles melts away.

Barb says, "This place is hopping!"

There are kids running around and people milling about. Horses and riders are coming in and going out to the surrounding trails that lead out to some nearby prairie land. Someone is harnessing a bushy-haired pony up to a buggy.

She had hoped to get away from so many people and bustle, but this all feels different. It's a calm busy. It feels comfortable.

Her dad says, "Plenty of space for all of us," and he immediately gets to setting up their home for the weekend.

Shelly helps set up camp, and when the last lawn chair is set around the campfire, she asks, "You need anything else? Want me to get firewood?"

"Naw, Shell. It's time to relax," her dad says, and she knows he knows that that doesn't mean *sitting around* for his little self-proclaimed gym rat daughter.

It means it's time for a run.

She dashes into the RV to change into some running shorts and a tank top. Quick as a wink, she heads out on a run while wrapping her blonde hair up into a ponytail. Medora's beautiful landscape and surreal beauty embrace her with open arms. Soon, she finds her rhythm – legs, arms, lungs, heart all in sync, all at peace in her own little world.

As she makes her way into the streets of Medora, she barely notices a truck with two guys driving behind her. She vaguely wonders why they are going so slow and don't just pass on by, but whatever. *Men.*

Jogging back into the Rancherama, Shelly stops to mingle with her dad's riding group and other visitors. The people here are just what the doctor ordered to ease her loneliness. Everyone is so cool and laid back, just having a good time. She doesn't even care that she's all sweaty and her ponytail is loose. She brushes away the strands of hair that dangle down the sides of her flushed cheeks.

Loaded with endorphins from her run, she smiles as she takes in the scene across the campsites. Then her eyes land on *him* – a tall, dark, handsome man standing a little slouched with a beer in his hand. He's talking with some other guys, about what? Who knows. All Shelly knows is that she wants to meet him.

She nudges Barb and asks, "Who's that guy over there?"

"Which guy? There are a bunch of them."

Shelly's eyes haven't moved. "The tall drink of water." She tips her head in the man's direction.

"Oh. *That* one," says Barb, and Shelly ignores the smile in her voice. "I believe that is Frank. Frank Kuntz."

"Frank Kuntz," Shelly says. She is smitten. "Well, I have *got* to know more."

"I don't know much about him," says her stepmom, "but I do know he's a single dad. His parents board their ponies here. They run the buggy rides concession every day during tourist season."

Shelly's wheels start turning, figuring out just exactly how she's going to get to know this *Frank Kuntz*. He always has people around him. It looks as though his girls are here too. It would not be cool to interrupt their family time.

While she plots her approach, a bunch of the campers start putting a campfire together. Then a few people get out some instruments. As the sun goes down, the fire crackles, the music plays, and the people visit. It is a lovely evening to gather around the fire and just enjoy the company of good people.

Then, as fate would have it, Frank happens to sit right down in the empty chair next to Shelly's dad. Perfect! It won't be awkward at all for her to look in that direction, a lot. While she enjoys the view, she sets about scheming how to get some one-on-one time with that handsome cowboy and find out more about him.

I could just wait everybody out as they slowly drift off to their campers until it's just him and me. She glances around and decides that will be her strategy, no matter how long it takes.

As though in on her plot, it doesn't take long for the crowd to start thinning. Shelly preps herself mentally. Her mind fills with questions for him.

Unfortunately, within minutes, Frank stretches and yawns. He says, "I'm beat. Think I'll hit the hay. It was very nice meeting you, Shelly."

She wonders if he can see her entire body deflate like a balloon let go. She manages, "Oh, sure. Yah." Fake yawn. "Me too." Even faker stretch. "I suppose my folks will want to get headed back to Bismarck early tomorrow morning. She gives him one last chance to see that this is likely his only opportunity to get to know her more.

Frank hesitates, looking at her and then the fire. He turns his head to the sounds of his daughters at their camper. They are giggling at first, then it turns into a squabble over something. That does it. Up he goes with a polite nod.

She knows almost nothing about him still.

The next morning while packing up, Shelly spots him. He is across the yard dealing with a foal. She wanders over casually to say goodbye.

Frank ties up the foal and stoops to milk a goat nearby. That's not a scene you see every day.

She asks, "What's her name?"

Frank sort of startles at the sound of her voice. "What? Who?"

"The goat. What's her name?" she repeats.

"Oh, her." He goes back to milking. "This is Myrtle. She's helping feed this little orphaned foal here." He nods his head toward the baby.

This is a perfect, distracting topic. As they talk, Shelly notices how he is with the animals. He is quiet and kind. His hands move calmly and confidently as he works. He doesn't seem to mind her keeping him company either.

By the time he finishes with his task, it looks like her folks are packed and ready to head out. She says, "I live in Minneapolis right now. If you ever get out that way," she gives her sweetest head tilt, "look me up."

He nods at the offer, but she can tell he's got an awful lot going on behind those handsome eyes.

Mystery swirls about him. So, she leaves it at that. If he is at all interested in her, he will just have to find her.

That assertion lasts no longer than the trip back to Bismarck. The whole trip she can't stop thinking of him. Besides, she had always been taught that, in matters of the heart, sometimes you have to take things into your own hands.

As soon as the RV stops in her folks' drive, she hurries inside and grabs a phonebook. She flips through the thin pages. "Linton, Linton, Linton. There!" Her finger trails down the K column searching for his name. "Ugh. Nothing."

She doesn't know the names of any surrounding towns he might be listed in, so she slaps the phonebook shut and plops onto a kitchen chair to think, think, think.

Then it hits her. "Medora!" she says out loud to no one. Medora is a *very* small town. Maybe she could send something to Frank there.

That's the new plan.

When she gets back to Minneapolis, she writes him a letter – complete with her address and phone number. The envelope reads: Frank Kuntz, General Delivery, Medora, ND. This might be her only chance to *maybe* find him again. Into the mail it goes.

Not many days later, lo and behold, Shelly receives a letter from a *Frank Kuntz*. Guessing by how recently she'd sent her letter, he must have written this one the same day he got hers!

She rips it open and devours the words – it's just his contact information – but they're *his* words written in *his* handwriting.

Then, Shelly Hauge, a grown woman and mother of two beautiful daughters, does the unthinkable. She picks up the phone, dials all but one of the numbers of his phone number, and like a schoolgirl, hangs up terrified.

This is crazy. What does she think she's doing? He lives hours away.

She dials again and hangs up again. And again. This happens many times.

By around 11 PM, she says to herself, "This is absolutely ridiculous. What's the worst that could happen? He hangs up on me, or he tells me he's not interested. And that will be that."

She takes a deep breath and dials the entire number. He answers immediately. He had been hoping she would call. Do they ever have things to talk about!

They talk until 6 AM when she realizes she has to shower and go to work.

All day long, she replays their conversation in her head. She had asked to hear the story of exactly her first letter had found him, and he told her how his daughters work at Medora's drive-in during the summer tourist season, and how they go to the post office at least once a day, looking for letters and news from boyfriends and others back home. Needless to say, the postmaster knows Frank and his family very well. His daughters had said the postmaster waved a little envelope in the air at them and, in a sing-song voice, said, "Girls, your *dad* got a letter!!"

She smiles, playing the whole night's conversation in her head over and over to keep it fresh and real. Especially the part when he told her that it had been *him* and his sixteen-year-old nephew in that truck driving super slow behind her on her jog through town. She blushes at how he'd said they were "enjoying the view" and "getting an eyeful."

After many similar night-long conversations in the days following, Shelly feels like she knows him so well finally, even though they had only met once.

Their letters maintain a constant flow in and out of their P.O. boxes. They talk long distance daily. Both their phone bills reach into the hundreds monthly. When neither can pay it, their service is cut off until they can scrape together enough money.

By Labor Day weekend, Shelly can't take it anymore. She decides to drive to Linton to see Frank.

At this point, it is no surprise that being with him in his element and with his family is easy and comfortable. It is full of laughter as well as serious talk about the future. She particularly loves it when he tells her about the Nokota horses – how his eyes light up and he gets all animated, waving his hands around and talking loudly. His passion for those horses is just one of the most attractive things about him. He draws her in, and she wants to stay.

Leaving Linton for Minneapolis is torture. She makes the trip nearly every weekend, leaving after work on Fridays. As though the universe wants to show her the beauty of what is happening in her life, her journeys are showered with the most stunning northern lights displays. She bathes in their beauty as they carry her to him.

On a crisp, clear October weekend, Frank drives Shelly to Surrender Hill, just west of Linton near the golf course. He stops the car and stares out the window for a moment, his hands grip and release the steering wheel. Shelly can tell he's got something big on his mind, but she waits quietly for him to say something.

Frank breathes deeply, looks her straight in the eyes, and takes her hands in his.

Her heart pounds so hard that she wonders if he can hear it. She looks straight back into his eyes and notices his breaths are quick like hers. The pressure of anticipation builds behind her eyes as she waits for him.

Finally, Frank says to Shelly, "Would you marry me?"

She's not exactly sure if he's done. He left the words hanging as though he had more to add, but that was it. He just looks at her with pleading, hopeful eyes.

She replies, "In a heartbeat," and lets the current of emotions carry her into his arms.

The very next day, Shelly looks for work in Bismarck and starts a new job there by January 1992. She spends as much time as she can with Frank, the girls, and the horses.

On September 12, 1992, Shelly marries Frank.

They are on their honeymoon to this day.

Chapter 17
Prairie Therapy

Peace is not something you wish for. It is something you make, something you are, something you do, and something you give away.
~ Robert Fulghum

2023

The sun hangs high over Frank as he stands in the middle of a couple hundred acres of prairie. *Grateful* is not a big enough word to describe how he feels. He is happy to put up shares of hay – splitting the hay he makes using his equipment with the person who owns the land – especially with this prairie. This is really good prairie which will make excellent hay for his horses. This is the kind of food source they know and love. It is an honor to offer it to them.

He leans on his truck and takes a moment to soak it in. Frank needs this for his mental health, today and every day. He needs to see the open stretches of land. He needs to hear the meadowlark's bell-like *pluk chup*, and the crane's prehistoric rattling bugle call. This time of year especially, he loves to watch the Vs of geese heading south, and listen to the flock's wings *shoosh shoosh* overhead, while the rest of his world is quiet.

With the sun and wind on his face, Frank looks forward to riding the rough terrain and feeling the satisfaction of his sickle mower slicing through long swaths of grass. He's been at it since the early morning hours and still has a day and a half of work to go. He is hungry and tired, but it all makes him feel alive. Doing these things for his horses, this is what makes getting up in the morning worthwhile.

He's had some rough mornings, as he does more often than not lately, grappling with his situation and fighting with his broken equipment. He's been angry. Especially when Christa got bashed on social media for daring to tell people about the land she found. Seeing her cry, or try to hide her tears, over anything – especially the horses – rips at his heart.

He's also fighting some ridiculous legal battles over the storage of some corral panels. He has zero time for these kinds of things and even less money to pay for it. Everything he's got goes toward caring for his horses.

When the dark hours of a rain-soaked day in the shed close around him, and the brandy seats itself in the darker corners of his mind, Frank starts to calculate all the things that have been taken from him and his family. Forty-five years of work, a complete and thorough registry, the logo his friends from Standing Rock designed, even the name Nokota, which Leo coined a lifetime ago, feels like it's been monopolized. Not to mention the money he has calculated he is owed for all the services and things he never charged for.

It's all enough to make a man – even a Kuntz – feel like giving up. He gets tired, so tired.

Thank God Christa and Shelly have already started up a fresh, new Kuntz Nokota Ranch registry. Jilly, the old mare who went to retire comfortably in Minnesota, was the first to start it up.

He will always have the Z4 brand on the right front shoulder. The new logo Christa has designed puts the 4 on the Z at the end of Kuntz. It's clever and fits well with the horse and rider silhouette. Unfortunately, during his lowest moments, it is all little consolation.

Autumn is near, and he still hasn't figured out how he is going to winter his herd on his little farm. He had vowed that his horses would not have to endure his small space again, but the prospect of buying land right now is dismal. That's not to say it might not still happen someday but by this winter? It's not going to happen.

They simply don't have the funds, connections, or support. Besides, these horses need hay.

Every day, these things and more roil and boil around in his mind.

For the last two weeks, however, his morning commute has been to this beautiful prairie, making beautiful hay for his beautiful Nokota horses. This is what makes him happy. He still finds joy in the hard work of saving the horses, no matter the cost and time. For Frank Kuntz, doing what is right sunup to sundown outweighs it all.

His phone rings and he sees it is Christa and the boys wanting to Facetime again. It's the third time today they have checked in on him. It's good to have someone looking out for you.

He swipes to answer with a big smile, "Hello everybody."

"Hey Dad," Christa sing-songs, "we thought we'd see how things are going out there. You having fun?"

"Oh yeah. Making good progress."

Beckett leans into the picture and says, "Wow, Grampa, you got a lot of dirt on your face!"

Frank acts surprised to hear this and touches his face. "I do? Oh my gosh! You're gonna have to hose me down when I get back tonight."

Beckett laughs at this excellent idea. Then the five-year-old says with seriousness beyond his years, "Grampa, I'm not proud of you."

Frank fake-blanches at that, but before he can come back with something clever, Beckett adds, "I'm *super* proud of you!"

That puts the most enormous smile on Frank's face. In the little picture of himself at the bottom of the screen, he can see his teeth gleaming against his dirty face.

He says, "Well, I thank you for that, Beckett. That means a whole lot."

Beckett beams, glad to have gifted that smile to his grandfather.

"That charged my batteries right back up. I guess that means Grandpa better get back to work."

Everyone waves as they close the call. His heart is full. The prairie awaits him.

The moment makes him want to share some of his happiness with those who care to hear about it, so he decides to make a video like Christa showed him how to do with his phone. It's been a long time since he's reached out to people on social media, and he knows many of his friends and followers are wondering how he is and what his situation is like at present. He hasn't had much good to say about anything or anyone lately, but today, he feels like sharing this slice of heaven.

He taps the buttons on his phone to record and says:

"Good morning. I thought I'd show you the morning commute I've enjoyed for the last two weeks." He pans the scene before him. "It's pretty out here. I love the plains. The beautiful skylines." He gets in the truck and turns down the old-time country music playing. "I'm very fortunate to be making hay for shares on this 200 acres of prairie. I'm about a mile in already." He keeps the video rolling while he drives, listens to the music, and decides what to say next.

"You know, I've spent a lifetime – my family and I have – saving a breed of horses. A unique geno/phenotype of a horse. Not for money. If we had been doing it for money, it wouldn't have happened. No way. Because you don't make money saving a breed of horses. Period. If you do, somebody, tell me how. I'd sure like to know."

He pauses as the truck hits some bumpy spots. He looks out at some cattle up by the windmill. Then the few mares he's been able to let graze out here come into view too. A little cloud shadows his thoughts now that he's started talking. His heartfelt honesty comes easily. "I think I've been screwing up the last 40 years. Never been easy. Always been a struggle. And the last several months have been a major struggle. There've been times when I felt like just walking away from everything. To hell with it. I don't need the work. I don't need the stress. You know? I don't need this. But I've been quiet. And I'm tired of being quiet."

He wrings his rough hands on the steering wheel then shifts his tone again. "Anyway, it's been a joy making hay out here. It's some of the best prairie hay you can make." He lets the landscape record for several seconds. "This is as positive and as pretty as it can get."

He presses stop. He'll get that on the social media channels right away. Maybe someone will listen.

Chapter 18
Progress and Struggle

Every struggle whether won or lost, strengthens us for the next to come.
~ Native American Proverb

1993-2000

Dressed in his best suit – his only suit – Frank stands next to his brother Leo on the steps of the state capitol building in Bismarck. They both look a little stunned.

"We got beat. They denied the horses *again*," says Leo.

Frank flips a hand at all the buildings around them. "The Nokota have been living on the plains of North Dakota long before any of *this* was here. They deserve to be the state's honorary equine."

Leo, thumbs hooked on his suspenders, looks up at the sky over the capitol grounds. His face is anchored in anger. Mad enough to spit, he gives Frank the impression he wants to just leave.

Frank looks out on the scene too. Remembering two years ago and how events had gone quite differently, he can understand why his brother looks so beaten down.

Back at their first attempt in 1991, the west chamber of the capitol building had been packed. Frank had heard earlier in the morning some of the politicians chuckling and calling it a *horse bill* and even a *Jackass thing*. They weren't taking it seriously. The legislative session had finally gotten to the Kuntz' lobbied bill that asked them to name the Nokota horse the state's official horse. Leo sat up in the balcony section, tense and nervous. On the house floor, Frank testified passionately and beautifully as always about the breed of horses he committed his life to.

"I speak for the horses," he had said. "I speak for them because they have no voice, and this breed – the descendants of Sitting Bull's war ponies – have been served an injustice many times over at no fault of their own except that they exist. I know these horses. I have learned their history as anyone here can through research, especially the excellent report entitled *The History and Status of the Wild Horses of Theodore Roosevelt National Park* by Dr. Castle McLaughlin. Believe me when I tell you, it is a rich and terrible history all in one. These horses have faced extinction and are threatened still today. The Nokota horses are living history. They deserve a future with proper recognition."

He went on to relay the highlights of the well-documented history behind his horses' origin. Frank knew he had to rely on the facts if he wanted to impact any politician's thinking. That's all anyone believes. Historical facts and documented evidence were his greatest weapon in the face of the legislation. Also there to support him were several other historians and professors – good people – who testified too.

If he and Leo could get the Nokota declared North Dakota's Honorary Equine, it might, just might, put a little pressure on the national park to stop their round-ups and think about what they were doing. The goal would be to get the park service to quit trying to change the DNA of those horses and let them live wild as nature intended.

When it had come time for the decision to be made, the senators and representatives practically laughed. They told the brothers they'd better "quit horsing around" and made demoralizing comments that mocked Frank and Leo's very existence at this session. They called the Nokota horses mutts and mongrels, and words like scam artists, hoodwinkers, and wannabe Indians hissed around the room like demons, as though the brothers should be ashamed of themselves for wasting everyone's time with such a meaningless plea.

Frank remembers watching his brother come down the steps looking like a whooped dog. On the ride home, Leo said, "The only other time I've ever felt so beaten down and worthless was when they were wheeling me into the hospital when I come back from Nam and all the protesters were whipping rotten fruit at me, calling me a baby-killer."

"I don't know what happened. I thought they were really listening. We'll try again next time."

Leo had ground his teeth and said, "Maybe next time, *Mr. Nokota*, you won't sound like such a huckster. They don't like the whole door-to-door salesman pitch, don't you know?"

That struck Frank at his core. *Huckster* is the *last* thing he ever has been or ever will be for the horses. A familiar hint of a fight flickered behind his dark eyes. After all, he never saw Leo itching to get up and talk in front of everyone on the horses' behalf. The look on Leo's face and the way he hung his head with his hands stuffed in his pockets, though, was a scene Frank will never forget. Not ever. He let the comment go.

That memory fuels his drive now, two years later. After presenting their excellent evidence once again, Frank and Leo get some air on the capitol steps as the session members take a break. Their bill has been shot down for a second time. Again, during the debate earlier in the House, one of the Democrats had made some comment about "wasting the State's time on such a frivolous bill."

Though Leo has let this repeated defeat kick him in the gut, Frank is not about to let go without a fight. "We gotta get back in there and hustle on the floor, Brother."

It doesn't take long before Frank learns that someone, a Republican, didn't like the rude comments that had been made about the Nokota horses either. He wanted to get back at the Democrats for making it, so he voted to bring the bill back up to be reintroduced.

This gives Frank an inkling of hope. "Let's find the people who voted against it the first time and try to talk them into voting for it the second time."

That is what the brothers do. They hustle on the lobby floor until they find enough people to listen to their plight for the horses' future.

This time around, the bill passes!

Leo reaches out to shake Frank's hand. "Brother, we did it. We really did it."

For a small moment, Frank lets the win give him hope. This is a victory! Right? But for some reason, his heart just can't embrace it.

"Leo," he says, "I know I should be happy, but it passed pretty much because the Republicans just didn't like what the Democrats said. Not on the merits of the horses themselves. It was about politics, not the horses."

Leo bolsters Frank. "I know it." He puts his arm over his brother's shoulders. "But let's take the win for now and celebrate. I'm buying."

* * *

Despite the title of North Dakota's Honorary Horse and all the begging and pleading Frank, Leo, and Castle do to try to convince the park to keep the original horses in the park, to allow their genetics to influence the herd, it is to no avail. Theodore Roosevelt National Park continues to round up and remove the "most Nokota-looking" horses and further try to "modernize" the park's horses.

Often, when Frank tries to talk to someone with the park service, it turns out ugly. If a person doesn't know him – understand his knowledge, background, passion, *and* stubbornness (and his promise) – it looks like he is just trying to antagonize. Regardless, the park maintains that its plan is the right way to go. Modernize the herd for the modern buyer.

Frank and Leo, however, manage to acquire several more highly impactful mares and studs for their breeding program.

On Auto and Bad Toe, Frank and his brother ride out to watch the gray alpha of one of the bands far, far out in the pasture at Pauline and Father Leo's ranch.

Frank pulls Auto to a stop and says, "Looks like Target out there is still one wild son-of-a-bitch."

Leo reins Bad Toe around and stops too. He shoves his short-brimmed hat high on his head and rubs his forehead. "That's about the size of it. Ain't nobody gonna take his mares, that's for sure."

Frank laughs, "He'll never settle down. No wonder the round-up ranchers hated him."

"Ya, they had it in for him, all right," says Leo. "He's lucky Castle found out they were gonna shoot him for stealing all the domesticated stallions' mares."

Frank adds, "Among other unsavory behaviors."

Leo's head bobs, "He had a target on his back, that's for sure. He owes that young lady a bit-o-gratitude, I'd say."

Frank watches Target stomp along the line of mares he's lording over. Rough-looking as they come, he is the quintessential wild stallion. With admiration, Frank says, "I'd say we do too. He is one amazing animal."

For a few minutes, they watch the stocky, thick-necked young stallion. Target's ever-present vigilance to protect his family makes Frank think of his own family and all they have been through lately.

At first, the newness of the Nokota breed kept sales up. Looking to the future, Frank had bought a section of his great-grandpa's place, but since then, he has lost it. They couldn't make the payments *and* feed the horses. Feeding the horses always takes priority.

As far as his place is concerned, foreclosure loomed on his doorstep for too long now. The time has come for it to be offered up in a short sale on the courthouse steps, but Frank is not about to let it go. He will find a way to save his home.

He swallows his pride, which is difficult for a Kuntz, and goes door-to-door to all of his neighbors and asks – no, *pleads* with them. "If you can find it in your heart, I ask that you not place a bid on my house at the short sale coming up. I'm hoping against hope that my brother Leo will be able to buy it. It's the only way we'll be able to keep the house and the land in the family."

All the neighbors know Frank and, for the most part, truly appreciate what he is trying to do for the horses, so it turns out that not many people show up for the sale, mostly curiosity seekers. Leo's bid – the only bid – takes it!

On the day Leo's check for the property is due, Frank says, "Okay, so now all we have to do is get your check from the Bank of North Dakota and then take it to the U.S. Marshall's office by 4:30. We can make that work, right?"

"Sure can," Leo says, cocksure he's got this in the bag.

They hustle up the steps together, go in, and hand over the check.

The attendant at the desk says, "ID please."

Leo takes out his tattered wallet and rifles through the cards.

Frank is antsy and starts tapping at the counter. It sure is taking his brother a long time to grab his driver's license. Finally, he asks, "What's the matter?"

Leo snaps his wallet shut and crams it in his back pocket. He thumps his hands on his hips and looks up at the ceiling. He will not make eye contact with Frank.

Frank asks again, nervous tension in his voice this time, "Leo. What is going on?"

Leo sighs and says with a cringe, "I don't have my driver's license."

"You *what*?!"

"You heard me. We gotta go back home and get it."

Frank looks at the time. "We'll never get back in time." He gives the clerk a pleading look.

The clerk behind the counter looks sympathetic but says, "I'm sorry, we close at 4:30. We can't make this transaction without a current photo ID. There's just no exception to that rule."

"We gotta make it work," says Frank. "Tell us what we can do to make this work."

The clerk looks into Frank's desperate eyes. He sees his sunken shoulders and genuine fear on his face. Both men look like they've missed a few meals, what with their sagging jeans and tired complexions. It is obvious these two men have seen their share of struggles in life.

Leo's frustration barks out, "It's *me*, I tell ya, I'm *Leo Kuntz*. Jeez, what do I have to do to prove it to you?"

The man at the counter sighs and gives a look of such consternation that Frank can tell they just might have a chance. Both he and Leo lean in with hopeful eyes.

"I suppose," says the clerk, "if you can get the bank to vouch for you – say you are who you say you are – then we can process your check."

"Easy!" exclaims Leo as he slaps the counter, showing his hand missing two fingers.

Frank gets his meaning and says, "And your oddball earlobe! You're easy as cake to ID."

It's true. The good folks at the bank know Leo well, including his unique physical features, and they are all too happy to vouch for him.

Frank and Leo get the check in just as the Marshal's office is closing up, and Leo "buys" Frank's place.

Which, technically, makes it Leo's place. That feels a little weird at times, but Frank and his family continue to live there, always with the hope of being able to buy it back eventually once things just turn around a little for them.

In 1996 a spark of hope for the Nokota is ignited when Peter Jennings with ABC World News does a special on Frank and Leo's struggle to preserve the Nokota horse and return them to the park. It draws positive attention for a while, but then that attention wanes, and the brothers are right back in the fight.

This life of saving a horse breed puts great strain on Frank and Leo's relationship. Their fights with each other over the little things (and the big things) become numerous, some heated, others suppressed only to fester and resurface at unexpected moments.

Right now, however – as the brothers check on Target's herd – is a good moment.

Target raises his head high in the air and curls his lip up to catch more scent in Frank and Leo's direction. Frank shakes his head, "Busted. He'll move 'em off now, I suppose."

They both get down and stand slightly hidden behind their horses. Maybe that will settle Target down. They want him to bring his band in a little closer so they can take a headcount and look for a couple of mares Leo hopes are in foal. The sun starts its descent as they wait quietly.

It brings to Frank's mind another evening he'd shared with his wife recently.

* * *

The frogs and crickets had just begun their nighttime songs as Frank and Shelly watched a mare and her foal have quiet time in the pen by the barn. The wind had finally subsided for the night, and a crisp, coolness blanketed the yard.

On a hill just past the barn, a few horses stood silhouetted against the dimming sky. Frank stared out at them, his mind heavy with thought.

"You know," he'd said to Shelly, "Castle's report shows how long these horses have been here. But I," he shakes his head, "I know I'm not a smart man with a fancy education or anything, but I have to believe they were here all along. Not 'introduced by the Spaniards' like every history book will tell you. The Spaniards came from the south. Those explorers had no clue what was up here on the northern plains already."

Shelly had only nodded and let him go on.

"I ask you to save these horses with me..."

She finished his sentence with, "Because it's the right thing to do."

The way she knows his thoughts always makes him smile. "That really is all there is to it." He'd gone back to watching the horses in the pasture – a little one was testing her legs and running circles around her mother. "And, for me, it's one small way to honor Lakota heritage after centuries of discrimination. I've always admired their ways, ever since I was a little kid." He paused before saying, "They want to revive their horse culture. I just know it."

On the horizon, storm clouds had begun to roll in. They darkened the sky and washed the evening with a bluish hue. Soft thunder rumbled in the distance.

"Did you know Castle's report also talks about how the blue roan is the color of the western sky? 'The domain of storms and warfare.' She says it's the Lakota belief that the colors of the West are blue and black. Riding a blue roan links a warrior to those powers." His voice was barely a whisper. "War ponies."

The blue roan mother in front of them made calm and soothing noises as she nuzzled her red roan foal. It was a magical bonding moment of love and trust.

Frank confided in his wife. "I sometimes wonder if Leo resents me."

Not completely surprised, Shelly had said, "Oh? Why do you say that?"

"I don't know. It's probably nothing. Just Leo being Leo. But," he paused, "the way he calls me 'Mr. Nokota' and says I just have to be in the spotlight." He looked to his wife. "It's all for the horses. Everything is for the horses. I don't *want* to be in front of the camera, but the horses can't speak for themselves. Somebody's got to do it. I'm that person. Leo doesn't know how to be that person. It's simply not who he is."

Shelly let the words rest. She has thought the same things for a while. It was good that Frank wanted to talk about it. Then she offered, "The two of you are so different."

"Always have been," Frank added. "Ever since we were kids. But it's like *because* we're so different it makes us a good team. I can't do *this*," he waved his hands to the corral and the pasture, "without him. We're so different, yet we need each other. But when he disappears for months at a time?" He stopped talking, looked at his feet, and shuffled some dirt. It is never his intent to talk about Leo behind his back.

Shelly finished his thought for him. "It's not fair, Frank. It's not right that he leaves the care of all his horses up to you and your parents and whoever else just happens to be around. We've got enough of our own to care for right here. Not to mention try to salvage whatever family time we can get with the girls."

"And there's just never any money. I'm so sick and tired of worrying about money." That had been all he could manage without breaking down.

Knowing he needed her words right then more than anything, his wife said, "We will figure something out. Something will come up. I have to believe it."

His eyes creased into a warm smile as he pulled her in. "My Shelly. Always in my corner." He remembers warmly kissing the top of her head. "What did I ever do to deserve you?"

She nestled into his shoulder and said with a smile in her voice, "I hunted you down, remember?"

* * *

"We need to find a way to make money," Frank says to Leo as they sort Black Fox into a holding pen with an open stock trailer backed up to it.

Leo sidesteps one way and Frank steps the other. Both brothers are quick and springy on their feet but remain loose and flexible. They watch the horse's ears twitch independently toward them or away. Frank makes eye contact only when he wants to urge the smaller black stud with a white sock in a certain direction. Leo anticipates each move Black Fox might even think about. Together, like a well-rehearsed, choreographed horse dance, without fuss or fight, the brothers ease their valuable stallion where they need him to go.

Frank says, "Trust me, Black Fox." He does a soft hop to the right, stands still, and then looks the black horse in the eye with a soft gaze. "You're gonna love where you're going." The horse moves in the direction he is asked. Frank looks down and steps away to create space. "Lots of pretty ladies are waiting for you."

The black Nokota stud with the white sock cooperates, although he never relaxes his thick neck and proud carriage. He is choosing to go quietly. If Black Fox didn't want to do what was being asked of him, it would be a very different scene, regardless of Frank and Leo's skill. He still remembers the terrors of the day he was captured, as well as the day he lost his mother. Scars like that never fully heal. Since he has been here, however, life has been good. There is plenty of grass, his family surrounds him, and he has found his place in the herd. Not to mention, he seems to be treated like a very special visitor every day. That gives him peace.

Stately and regal as a king, Black Fox steps into the trailer. He does not startle at the clanging sound his hooves make. He's a sensible stallion with a level head. Besides, this is not the first time these two-leggeds have asked him to get into the metal tunnel. Last time, they took him to a wide-open space with hills to climb and water running through it. The bonus was a band of mares waiting for him.

Leo closes the trailer and hops up on the fender to see that the stud is settled. Frank is thankful to have his brother back from the couple-month stint working as an assistant wrangler out in Montana at the Silver Tip Ranch deep inside Yellowstone National Park.

"I know," he finally responds to Frank. "I been thinking about that. I might-a made a connection with someone who can help us out. He and his wife seem real interested in our horses and their story. I don't have to remind you what an exclusive place that is. Only the super-rich and super-connected go there. I'm lucky my buddy got me that summer gig."

Frank does not need to be reminded of the amazing opportunity Leo landed. Frank also does not need to be reminded how rich the Silver Tip Ranch's clientele must be to secure a couple of weeks a year out there. It is a private ranch so secluded in the heart of Yellowstone National Park that you have to either fly in or ride in over extremely rough roads. Hardly anybody even knows it exists. Naturally, Leo had brought two of his horses with him. There's no better *doing* horse than a Nokota horse.

Leo hops down and leans against the trailer with his thumbs hitched on his suspenders. "Fleischmann's their name. Charlie and Blair. They're top-notch horse people from Pennsylvania. You should've seen the way they handled themselves on a horse. Really big into horses. Hunters. Eventers. Charlie's one of those steeplechase jockeys and coaches too. From what I can tell, they're good people, like genuinely *good* people. You know what I mean?"

Frank is skeptical but he says, "Okaaay. So why do you think they might be able to help us?"

"Well," says Leo, fully expecting his younger brother to question his opinion, "Charlie really took to the two Nokota I brought. He says to me one day coming in from a long one, 'Those sumbitches came back the same way they went out. No need to swap out Nokotas,' and I says to him, 'Nope sir, Nokota'll run circles around any of these other breeds.' So we got to talkin' and he says he and the little woman would like to come visit us here in North Dakota to see more of our horses and learn about them."

That makes Frank raise an eyebrow. He loves it when people show interest in the horses. Frank, Leo, and Castle have pretty much been the only ones promoting and advocating for this breed's preservation. It would be good to get some more supporters, especially if they've got connections and know-how.

After a moment's thought, Frank says, "We've been talking for a while now about how we need to form some kind of organization to get some help. A family foundation or something. And you and I both know, if these Fleischmanns come for a visit, the horses will sell themselves."

Leo smiles and pats the trailer. "We do know it, indeed."

Black Fox whinnies and snorts in agreement.

* * *

On a high ridge overlooking a sweeping valley, Frank, Shelly, Leo, Charlie, and Blair sit on rocks or crouch in the grass as they watch Black Fox with his band. They had left their four-wheelers a ways back and walked up here so as not to spook the herd.

"They're amazing animals, with an amazing story," says Charlie Fleischmann.

"Mmhm," say the brothers in unison, looking at the horses in the distance.

Blair sweeps her hair to the side against the wind. "Leo told us all about them, and we were so impressed with the two he brought to the Silver Tip, but this ..." For a moment, as so often happens when a visitor experiences the herd for the first time, she seems at a loss for words. "This is magical."

Shelly says, "It's impossible to explain what it feels like to be with the Nokota. You really do have to experience it for yourself." She knows this from personal experience.

After taking a moment to process, Charlie asks, "What are your intentions with them? What is your goal?"

That's an easy one for Frank. "Well, we want to propagate in a way that preserves their past *and* their future. We would love to find a sanctuary where they'll always be protected and people can come to see them and learn about them. And, somehow, we would love to get some of them back to their people, the Hunkpapa Lakota."

Leo adds, "We know we need to create some kind of foundation."

Blair asks, "Like a non-profit organization?"

Leo goes on, "Yeah, something like that so we can keep doing this." He sweeps his hands out across the land and the herd. "But that kind of business stuff isn't much our strong suit, and we're running outa money. I don't know if you know this," he gives a side-grin as he looks at her, "but there's no money in saving a breed of horses."

Frank shakes his head. "Nope. We're not in this to make money for ourselves. It's for the ponies. *Always* for the ponies."

Shelly interjects, "But we're quick studies. We need some guidance to get going. So many people want to help, they just don't know how."

Frank adds, "Shelly's really good at all the computer stuff and excellent with administrative responsibilities." He worries that this will put a strain on her insurance job, but he also knows that when his wife puts her mind to something, there's no stopping her.

Blair looks at her husband and says, "They need a non-profit."

Charlie says to his wife, "Sounds like they do." He looks at the others with a light in his eye and says, "We happen to be well-versed in this. Let us help you guys launch."

* * *

For the year of 1999, Frank's life is filled with all the things it takes to create a non-profit organization designed specifically to save a horse breed. The learning curve is huge!

The little team finds some office space in Linton where Shelly, Castle, Charlie, and Blair will work. Charlie finds some software that is perfect for setting up a registry. He puts in many long hours taking the horses' paperwork and transferring the details of each horse into the program.

Shelly quits her insurance job so she can focus solely on this mission. She exercises her office skills by keeping all the administrative elements organized, quickly assumes the role of secretary and treasurer, and even generates a fresh, inviting website. Castle helps her design the website, writes up the breed standards, and creates a summary of the Nokota history.

Blair Fleischmann does what it takes to file with the IRS for non-profit status. Having already been involved in a lot of causes and issues in their hometown in Pennsylvania, this is her wheelhouse. She takes charge of the organization's structure. She knows how 501(c)3s work, how to set them up – all the laws and regulations. She figures out what committees they will need and how to get permission for this and that.

They all attend countless meetings about all the details. What categories of horses would they have? How will the horses get registered? What requirements should they have for registering a horse? What will the forms look like?

Castle, at one point, brings her friend Butch Thunderhawk from the park service and the United Tribes College into the conservancy. Being a teacher of traditional Native American Arts, he designs a logo that represents the beauty and tradition of the Lakota culture.

Finally, after hundreds of hours of preparation, The Nokota Horse Conservancy is granted official non-profit status by the Internal Revenue Service.

By now, Charlie and Blair have carefully selected two horses from the herd to take home to Pennsylvania. In Chester County particularly, their horses naturally excel in the fox hunt and paper chase obstacle courses for adults and kids alike, demonstrating the utility of Nokota in the field so much that it piques curiosity. Charlie's mother even decides to buy a number of Nokotas to train and keep on her Virginia estate. She hosts several fund-raising activities for the Nokota Horse Conservancy that help it get off the ground.

With the Fleischmann's many affluent connections, and all the people getting involved and becoming members and officers, word gets around. Together, they reach out to promote the horses and gain new supporters and owners.

For Frank, the best part of it all is that the horses sell themselves on their own merits. Through hearing their story and seeing them in person, people are inherently inspired to help these horses. That gives Frank hope. Often it all feels like a whirlwind – so many others are now involved in what used to be intimately his and Leo's – but this fight is about something so much bigger.

Plus, as though to put the final punctuation mark on the quest to save the Nokota, yet another round-up is held at the Theodore Roosevelt National Park during which the last Traditional Nokota is removed – 9007 they call him. Nokota Horse Conservancy supporters purchase 9007 along with a few others. Frank and Leo have saved as many descendants of Sitting Bull's ponies as possible. Now, it is time to get about the business of preserving their future.

News of the Nokota is out! From exclusive ranches in Montana to a strong Nokota community on the East Coast, recognition and awareness can only bring good things for the breed. Right?

Chapter 19
Clinics

Memory is the diary that we all carry about with us.
~ Oscar Wilde

2023

The road to Chester Springs, Pennsylvania is long and restless. Frank's legs get wiggly from sitting so long. His sister Patty and nephew Brandon keep him entertained for the most part. They all take turns driving a part of the 23-hour trek, but his two sidekicks are dozing at the moment.

Frank checks his side mirrors. The trailer stretching behind him carries precious cargo. The few young mares and studs are traveling well, even the two untouched boys from Standing Rock Reservation. Nokota horses usually do. They get their rear ends turned around in the trailer, pick a manageable stance to settle into, and find comfort in being close to their brother or sister for the long journey.

Watching the countryside slide by, Frank settles his mind on them. It is always hard to pick and choose who will stay and who will go. He knows every one of his horses so well. Selecting and removing them from the herd is like sending away a child. That feeling of loss will never change, but knowing where they are going makes all the difference. He knows that Christine McGowan's non-profit Nokota Preserve clinic will be the right place for these few horses to find their forever home. The clinics here have always been held in a way that helps auditors and participants learn how the Nokota horse is so different from a domesticated breed.

These clinics are one of the main reasons the Nokota community on the East Coast still thrives today as it did back when the Conservancy was first formed. Many people have come and gone in the meantime, as they often do, but everyone who has played a part in contributing to the preservation of the Nokota horses' future is an important building block. Without that support, who knows how he and his brother would have managed?

A light rain speckles the windshield. The darkness of night approaches. Frank flicks on the windshield wipers and lets their rhythmic beat bring back memories of many clinics gone by.

He has promoted the Nokota breed in clinics and expos all across the country, several in Texas, and many right in Linton. He brings young horses to be worked with and up for potential sale to the right person. That's always the neatest part. Watching one of the horses find their person. It can happen in all sorts of different ways depending on the individual, but when the connection happens, well, it is unmistakable.

Hands-on experience guided by a clinician helps build a foundation for those who have never handled a relatively untouched, young horse. The horses Frank brings to clinics often have had very little contact with humans. He knows from years and years of experience, whether with a newborn foal or a gelding who hasn't found his person yet, that first touch can be an important part of the Nokota bonding experience. The horse and the human must build trust and respect before they can think about things like ropes and halters.

Clinicians, Frank has learned, each have their own unique styles and often a personal agenda to sell something, whether it's a mindset, a product, or their ego. He insists anyone who works with the Nokota focuses on the horse's natural language, like what they naturally do to communicate with each other out in the wild. A Nokota herd's communication is full of body language and eye contact. It is clear, compassionate, and honest as the day is long.

Memories of Black Fox, gone almost twenty years now, come to Frank's mind. He was gentle with his mares and fiercely protective of his foals. He would risk life and limb to keep his family safe, even when it meant intruding on another stud's band to get a stray little one from his own band back to its mother. He could posture his small frame in such a way that would make other stronger, faster stallions quake at the sight of his bulging, rock-hard muscles and his snorting, pawing, prancing, and pacing. His intent, whether fierce or friendly, was always precise and clear, but never more than necessary. That stallion was peaceful yet strong, wise yet carefree, old when young, and youthful when old.

Trainers have to be that way too. Call it *natural horsemanship* or *reaching out* or *horse whispering* or whatever you want. If you don't speak the Nokota language, you may be able to force some things to happen, but it won't last. It won't be real.

Oftentimes, people just come to the clinics to audit. As onlookers, they watch the transformations from the other side of the pen, maybe under a shade tree or canopy set up, and write their poems and stories or draw and paint. Whatever inspiration the process brings to them.

Frank tends to watch clinic events unfold from a distance. He positions himself so that he has a good view – on a fence rail, in the shadows, or sitting on a hillside, camera in hand. He has watched all sorts of relationships form between his horses and clinic participants. It is rewarding to witness the humans learn as many new things as the horses during the whole process. Some take minutes to develop. Others take days.

The horses, in a very honest way, help strong-minded (and strong-willed) men and women learn how to humble themselves. Timid people who have been through a wide array of life's struggles rediscover the confidence they once had or discover strengths they never knew they had. It is a beautiful thing watching the learning, the breakthroughs, and the bonding.

There are times, however, when Frank ducks out altogether, especially when clinicians or landowners start to hustle a bunch of their products and hype up their property. He's not a fan when the whole thing becomes too much of a show to benefit an ego or gain profit that doesn't benefit the horses. It's hard for him to watch when it turns into something that isn't all about the horses.

Not to mention these events – clinics, expos, what-have-you – are expensive to put on and a lot of work, particularly when he hauls horses all the way to Texas. He knows the events are great for the horses, but he doesn't make much off of them unless he sells a horse. Often, he barely covers expenses.

Once in a while, a truly magical moment occurs. Like the time a tough-as-nails Minnesota man named Russ came to a clinic, mostly to support his wife as she worked with a horse she planned to buy. She had raved and gone on at home about *the magic of the Nokota* since the day they'd met. Anytime she talked about this breed's story, he could see how she fought back tears. So Russ figured it was time to check out what all the fuss was about.

With shoulders so wide his arms couldn't even hang straight down, and a brow looming over distrustful, skeptical eyes, Russ made it clear that he was just here because his wife wanted him to be. After Frank visited with the couple for a while and got to know them a little, Frank had a feeling. He gets those a lot. They're usually dead-on accurate. This man, like so many, had his own story, full of troubles and betrayals, but here he was for his gal. Deep down, Frank had a hunch he'd come for himself too.

So, Frank decided to bring Red Eagle to the clinic.

Red Eagle, a stout and stunning five-year-old, strawberry roan overo gelding with a blonde Fabio-style mane and tail, had been worked with on other occasions, but he was stand-offish and never made a whole lot of progress. He never made a good connection with anyone. This horse's outer shell was tough. Tough-as-nails. When approached, a little white showed in the gelding's eyes – distrusting, skeptical.

That year – the hot, dry summer of 2021 – the Conservancy had enlisted Anna Twinney as the clinician. Frank liked her style and her way with the Nokota. She gets it – how you have to listen to the horses. She understands that even though the horses don't speak with words, they speak volumes in so many other ways. He liked how she could adapt to each person too. No matter the circumstance, she could find a way to help them and show them how to reach their assigned horse in a meaningful way. She was also good at dealing with the variety of emotions and personalities the participants brought to the table. These are some of the things Frank looks for in a trainer. None of that old-style cowboy nonsense. That never works out with a Nokota – at least, not in a way that creates a lasting friendship.

The clinic area had been set up outdoors, a ring of several small working pens, each with a bucket of water and an easy-out opening. The pens were made from six-foot-high fence panels creating a huge circle where people could view the process. Volunteers helped get all the horses sorted and situated into individual pens.

Once separated from the other horses, Red Eagle was a coiled spring inside his cell. He paced and pranced. He snorted and scraped the dirt. Before anyone could do a thing about it, he launched himself straight into the air until his front feet hung over the top rail. Then, with a phenomenon of athleticism, his rear legs caught the top rail too. Hanging over the panel, he writhed and wrenched his body until he untangled himself and escaped to the center of the ring, virtually unscathed. He'd made it clear he didn't want to be there.

Eventually, with Anna's coaching, the volunteers brought Red Eagle back. This time, he chose to stay. Then, under Anna's watchful eye, Russ came in and the two began the process of getting to know each other.

Watching from a tented area, Frank noticed something different happen between the gelding and the man as they navigated the basics together: stick and string, rope with loop, give to pressure, halter. When the two were together, both grew quieter and gentler – eyes, body, and energy. Shoulders sank. Movements slowed. Eyes softened. When at first, Red Eagle always turned his rear to Russ, the gelding learned to slowly turn to angle his neck and chest for scratches. It was evident, and not just to Frank but to the rest of the clinic's participants looking on, that these two were good together.

On the second to last day of the clinic, Russ planned to go on a tour with a few others, but when he headed for the truck just out of Red Eagle's sight, the muscle-bound gelding started raising a holy tantrum in his pen. No one could calm him down. He was about ready to jump out again! Everyone hollered for Russ. Someone ran to catch the truck about ready to leave.

"Russ, your horse needs you!" they said with an urgency that somehow, without knowing details, made perfect sense to this man. Without hesitation, he quick-stepped back to Red Eagle, put his hands in the air, and spoke to him in the soothing tones they'd both become accustomed to in the last few days. Almost instantly, Red Eagle settled down. But it was more than that. As Russ stood resting his arms on the rail, Red Eagle tipped his head to look him straight in the eye. Chest still heaving a little, Red Eagle gazed into his eyes.

Russ said to him, "Easy, boy. You and me. We're the same. I'm not gonna leave you." The words came low and gruff and one hundred percent from the heart.

Red Eagle, never breaking eye contact, took in a massive breath and let it out in one, long, nostril-fluttering sigh.

The horses see and react to what is real, no matter what kind of façade a person tries to put on. You can't lie to a Nokota.

Frank had been taking in the whole scene from the sidelines. Now he knew what he had to do.

Once the other participants had dissipated and gone back to their own tasks, Frank got up and went to stand next to Russ still leaning on Red Eagle's pen. He'd seen everything he needed to see.

"I believe that horse needs to go home with you," he said.

When the tough-as-nails man turned, Frank saw the tears that had already begun to fall, and when those brutish arms locked him in an embrace, Frank hugged back.

On the last day, Anna Twinney said she couldn't help thinking that this man and this horse had been best friends in another life. It was a vision she simply could not shake. The universe had finally reunited them over time, space, and worlds.

Red Eagle had found his person.

Those are moments Frank treasures. Those kinds of people sharing the Nokota world with him make the long hours and the countless miles all worthwhile.

Darkness has settled over the highway now. Headlights and taillights reflect on the glossy wet road as the occasional trucks and cars pass by. The humming tires threaten to lull him to sleep, so he switches on the radio and turns the volume way down as he searches for a decent station. He could wake Brandon to have him take a shift, but Frank's mind is too active to sleep right now anyway. The next stop for fuel won't be for another hour or so.

In the cab's dimness, he checks the map lying next to him folded open so he can see which highway exit he should be looking for. He chuckles to himself at the thought of how everyone gives him a hard time for still using a clumsy paper road map instead of his fancy phone to find his way. Why change when it still makes sense?

He's looking forward to this clinic. Autumn in Pennsylvania is so beautiful. Christine always makes him and his family feel welcome and loved. He is fortunate to have people like her in his life, especially now.

The glow of the dashboard and the truck's rhythm bring his memory back to this same trip in 2021. That hot, dry summer had evolved into a full-on drought year. The 90 acres or so the landowner had allotted to the horses was getting down to pretty much wheat stubble and weeds. In drought years, that is often the case. He had hay, though. The conservancy had hay. He remembers asking to start feeding hay, particularly because he was about to head out East for a couple of weeks to promote the Conservancy through a few events, including this clinic. Frank also worried because, in years like this, there is often only one water source, a waterer up by the yard. Everything was deathly dry that summer. Creek beds dried up for the most part. He'd hated leaving the herd, especially since his right-hand Jennifer wasn't allowed on the land due to her fairly hefty personality conflict with the landowner. He had to go, though, and he was assured that the herd would be handled just fine while he was away.

The whole trip out east he had a funny feeling. It niggled at the back of his mind so much that eventually he called Shelly and Jennifer and asked them to go check on the horses.

They did.

The pump – and it still makes his heart ache and his stomach sick to think of it – had gone out at some point, and over the course of those two weeks he was gone, they had lost ten horses. The available hay had not been fed, and the horses hadn't had enough to drink.

Frank grips the steering wheel harder as he remembers the conversation he'd had when he got home.

"Frank," said the landowner, "There's something wrong with your horses. They're droppin' like flies."

Frank remembers feeling like he'd been punched in the gut by an opponent he couldn't punch back. He'd felt accused of doing something to his horses that was making them weak.

Always walking on glass, what with the rent money he still owed, all he could say was, "I don't think there's anything wrong with my horses. I've never experienced this before."

Then his memory fast-forwards to the same time, the same trip the next year. This time, about four days before he left, he and Jennifer went in and pulled out twenty or so mares to bring home. They went through all hundred and eighty or ninety head, sent them through the corrals a few at a time, and picked the ones that looked a little thin or ones they just weren't quite certain could handle much stress. They pulled them out and brought them home to put them on full-feed.

He knew the rest of the horses were going to be put in the sunflower field – which had some grass but not enough by Frank's standards – at some point while he was away, so again he asked that the landowner start feeding hay. He was assured all would be taken care of.

About three days into his trip, he called to say they really needed to start feeding the horses hay, and again was assured all was fine. This time, Frank didn't want to risk it. He called Jennifer and told her to walk in the back way really early in the morning to check to see if the horses had food. When she reported back that "they ain't being fed at all," he called the landowner again but was met with the same thing as all the other times.

Frank decided to have Jennifer sneak hay from his own yard in that back way to the horses. As far as he could tell, it was almost two weeks before anyone noticed.

A bump in the road jostles his mind back to the here and now. He shakes his head to rid his mind of the memories and takes a deep, cleansing breath. This time, he knows exactly where his horses are and who and how they are being cared for, albeit still in the crunched space on his little farm. They are safe. They are fed. They are loved.

Though he wishes so many good things for the ponies – like hundreds of acres to roam and graze like a time so long ago – bringing them to his little place, in reality, feels liberating. He and his family are free to seek a permanent home, and they will care for these horses the best they can, always working toward the next opportunity that gets them a little bit closer to that ultimate goal.

The sun rises over the rolling landscape as they drive past the half-moon Nokota Horse Preserve sign hanging at the long driveway's entrance. It is a pretty scene of fence lines leading toward a red-roofed barn and white house tucked within a bank of trees just beginning to turn the vibrant hues of fall. The sky is crystal blue with puffy cotton clouds.

He would like to get out and stretch his aching joints from sitting so long, but Frank just rolls down the window, takes in the crisp autumn air, and waves to his host as she comes from the barn. Then he pulls into the yard and drives through the arena opening to do a huge turnaround in order to back up to the pens Christine has already put up in the normal spot for unloading the Nokota.

There are already plenty of people there. Every time he comes to visit, he is greeted by old friends, and some new ones, all excited to see him and the Nokota horses he has brought for the clinic.

Getting the horses from the trailer to the pens is always a special moment for Frank and everyone involved. The horses need to be funneled up a little hill to get to the pens, but there's no fencing on either side, so all the people stand on the sides and basically make a human chute.

Frank swings the trailer door wide. Patty, ponytail bobbing, jogs her tiny frame to the other side and holds it open. Two mares stand at the opening with their heads low and their ears pricked forward. It's typical for a Nokota to take a moment to evaluate the situation before stepping out of a trailer. These two are no exception. Those behind wait patiently.

A woman, eyes wide as saucers, stands next to Patty. Frank hears the lady say to his sister, "So we just stand here? And they'll go up to the pens? I feel like I should be holding a whip or something, just in case."

Patty looks up at the tall, slender woman, smiles, and replies in her deep, husky voice, "Well, it won't work if we send out the wrong kind of energy. You gotta take a breath and relax hun." She motions how to do this, and the woman models it back at her. "That's right. Now stand calm and confident. You just wish on these ponies all the good things you can think of, and they'll know you, like all of us here. It won't take them but a second to figure out we're their biggest fans."

The woman looks a little skeptical but willing. Patty winks at her and softly nudges her arm with her shoulder then breathes deeply and closes her eyes. When Patty peeks, she sees the woman has closed her eyes too. She looks across to her little brother, and she and Frank share a knowing glance as the first mare steps softly out of the trailer.

Then the rest follow. All is quiet, save the rhythmic thuds of hooves. The horses hold their snorts and whinnies as they swing their heads respectfully to the people lined up along either side. Even the birds have silenced their songs for this magical moment. Like a royal procession, one by one, the Nokota walk between the human fences, up the hill, and into their pens.

Frank watches, along with all the spectators, as the horses get settled. The giant round bales await. Fresh water too. After this long journey, the ponies just want to roll and stretch and lie down for a while. It doesn't take long for all the horses to relax and settle in. Even the two boys from Standing Rock. All have hay, water, and each other.

It's time for hugs and handshakes, pictures, and lots of questions about the trip.

Waiting patiently, well off to the side, stands Christine. She loves watching Frank with his fans. Every time he comes back, it's like Christmas with her favorite person. Seeing him again after so much time has passed sweeps her memory back to the time she first met Frank. It is a memory she holds dear and so very close to her heart and will stay with her forever.

It was nearly a decade ago now at a clinic in Ohio.

The domestic horses Christine gave English riding lessons on were having health issue after issue, especially with their legs and feet. She just could not keep the horses sound.

When her neighbor introduced her to their Nokota horses, that was it. Christine became obsessed with the breed, not only because of their health and hardiness but because of their temperament. These horses were interested in people. That's what she wanted for her horse-crazy daughter, so she packed up her truck and trailer and traveled to Ohio with her seven-year-old son and ten-year-old daughter to an all-mare clinic where they would begin their own little Nokota journey.

She'll never forget it. There she was, all dressed in her English riding equipment and attire, while everyone else wore western-style clothing and tack. While she and her daughter Neva wore jodhpurs and their little velvet riding helmets, everyone else donned kerchiefs, belt buckles, and cowboy boots. She had never felt so awkward and out of place in her entire life, but they welcomed her warmly. Besides, she was there for a purpose, to learn. She worked her tail off in the blazing sun all through that clinic.

A couple of days into the clinic, she was exhausted. At one point, she looked over to where her boy Keegan sat curled up sleeping in a chair next to a stack of books he'd brought. He'd been such a trooper and so very patient, and she needed to shield him from the sun, but like everyone else in the clinic, she was carefully navigating a situation with the horse she was working with. She kept glancing nervously over there, painfully aware that her son needed her, but she couldn't get to him.

Then, came Frank.

Christine knew this was Frank Kuntz, but she hadn't yet met him in a way to know anything about him. Regardless, there went Frank. He walked across the noisy commotion of the arena, left the arena, took his light denim jacket off his back, and then, with the love only a father can know, oh-so-gently and tenderly put it around her sleeping son.

At that moment, Christine felt she knew this man better than some people she had known her whole life. From then on, she no longer felt like a stranger in a strange land. This simple gesture made her feel like family.

Now, her mind's eye sweeps her back to the present, and she feels the smile her first memories of Frank bring her. She chuckles, too, at the memory of bringing home not one, but two mares from that clinic, the start of her Nokota journey.

Frank, caught up in a group conversation, sees Christine waiting on the sidelines and politely excuses himself to go to her. She wraps her arms around him like she would a favorite uncle.

"It's good to see you," he says.

Christine holds him at arm's length and says, "You too, my friend."

Then she launches into some details about what's happening when, and where he should be, and whatnot. He leads her back over to the horses so he can watch them.

Patty joins them at the rail and points to the two young studs from the reservation's herd. "So those two are handling the trip nicely. I know they haven't been handled yet, but I have a feeling they'll do just fine. They're going somewhere special?"

"Yup," Frank bobs his head. "John is sending them to be part of an equine therapeutic program."

Christine adds, "By the looks of how they're handling this whole trip, I'd say they're going to be pretty amazing at it."

They watch the young studs. The little black one has his face stuffed right down inside the round bale in the feeder, while the other lies nearby stretched out on the bedding, his belly facing out, content as can be.

Patty says thoughtfully, "Your friend John is pretty special to you, isn't he?"

Frank doesn't take his eyes off his friend's colts and takes a minute before he answers. "He's more than a friend. He believes these horses should get back to the Hunkpapa at some point, like I do." Frank chuckles, "The first time I met him, he came up to me and said, 'Thanks for taking care of *our* horses.' We've been friends on a mission ever since. When he called me his brother one day, I called him brother back, so we're more than friends."

Patty smiles softly and nods. Then she leans over the fence rail. "So all these ones are spoken for?" She knows how hard it is for her younger brother to say goodbye to every horse, but she also knows how much hay he has to buy to feed the rest of the herd at his place this winter. Selling horses is just part of the deal.

Christine says, "Most of them. I have a feeling they'll all find a good home before the event is over."

Even though he hates comparing a horse to a dollar amount, when he calculates how much each horse costs to raise from foal to adulthood – feed, vet bills, and such – he is confident in the price he expects. In his mind – at least in the cases of the younger ones – the new owner is really just paying him for taking care of their horse up to the point when they found each other.

Brandon comes over as their little group wanders over to watch the mares.

Patty asks, "You about ready to head out?"

Brandon replies, "I got a little time before I have to go."

As soon as Frank leans over the top wooden rail, an overo dun comes right over to him.

"Hey there, Muddy," Frank says. He scratches her shoulder which she has positioned perfectly for him to reach.

Brandon leans against the fence too and asks, "Muddy? This is Fiona."

Frank keeps scratching the mare's shoulder. "It is Fiona. I just call her Muddy because of her story."

Patty smiles and rests her back against the fence. She nestles her hands in her pockets and says, "Tell the story, Frank. Can't believe Brandon hasn't heard it yet."

Frank is happy to tell it.

"Well, back in 2019 at the land we used to rent, I always went out to check the mares every day. I noticed a black mare off in the distance by herself pacing. When I got there, I found a hole dug in the ground where the landowner had been digging for gravel. The hole was filled with deep, thick mud, and," he pats the mare, "this newborn girl right here."

Muddy lets out a deep sigh and lets her eyelids go lazy. She's heard the story many times.

Brandon's eyes go wide. "She was stuck in there? Just born?"

"Yup, and man was she a-fightin'. I tried to pull her out, but the mud was too dense and kept sucking her in. So I called for backup. All I could do while waiting was unpack the mud stuck in her nose and her mouth. There was so much mud in her mouth and nose that I wasn't sure how she was even breathing."

Patty adds, "It's amazing she's alive. Can't even believe it."

"Believe it," says Frank. "Anyway, it wasn't long until Jenn and my grandson Colten came to help rescue this little fighter. Together, we pulled her out. She was weak, tired, and caked in thick, wet mud. Muddy."

She swishes her tail and turns one ear toward Frank at the sound of her name.

Patty says, "She's a sweetheart. Curious and loves people."

Franks thinks for a moment as he gives Muddy a final pat. "I've always kind of thought she seems grateful to humans. For saving her and all. You know?"

Brandon gives this some thought and reaches for Muddy to sniff his hand. She wiggles her big lip over his knuckles then lets him rub her face all the way up to her ears.

Frank's nephew smiles softly and says, "She's going to make someone a really great friend, isn't she."

There is no question.

Finally, Patty breaks the moment with, "Who's hungry? I'm cooking!" and she trots off with Christine to the house where she will help whip up her typical professional chef-style meal.

The clinic goes on.

An exuberant French girl, whom Frank remembers meeting almost a decade ago in Texas, works with the little mare he has brought for her named StarLight. This young lady, full of energy, ambition, and kindness, had wanted to buy a horse from him and Leo back then and have it shipped to her home in France, but the details, logistics, and price got in the way.

She had shown genuine concern when she asked about his herd and his situation at home. He was happy to bring StarLight here for her. Frank really enjoys seeing the horse-human relationship start to unfold. It's one of the best moments in the gentling process.

A day or so in, after a session, he asks her, "So how are you feeling about everything?"

It was a simple question, but Anouchka has been holding a lot of thoughts in. She starts to expound, in her thick French accent, all at once. "Well, if I'm going to be truthful, I am not super happy with how Starlight is responding to the training. I don't know if it's the right ... emm ... how you say ... style? For her, I don't think it is working. But did you see how she keeps going to my daughter over to the side there? This horse loves my four-year-old baby girl, Frank. It's the most special thing. I can't explain it with the right words. Even my husband sees. All I know is that I have to take this horse with me. I don't even know where I am going to put her. We move back to France in one more year."

Frank just blinks as she takes a weepy breath. Then he says with his most soothing, sensible tones, "How about we just worry about the here-and-now for a minute, hm?"

Her big eyes look at him with trust and hope.

"You say you aren't sure the style is right for Starlight?"

"Yes. I don't know, but at times it just feels not right. Em ... too rough, maybe, for her. Not enough like the horses think."

Frank has been thinking the same thing. Pressure and release. Some of the horses take to it okay, but some don't.

Anouchka goes on. "Sometimes I think it would be nice if I could do it my own way. My own style. Wouldn't that be neat, Frank? To have a clinic of our own style where each horse is trained in the way it needs?"

Frank has thought this very same thing for years. He nods and says, "Absolutely. That would be the perfect clinic to me."

Anouchka is quiet for a moment. Then her eyes light up like the star on a Christmas tree. "Frank! That's it!"

He's startled by her sudden shift in mood, but he's listening.

"Where is Christine?" Anouchka asks. Her energy hums with excitement.

Christine, finishing a conversation with another guest, raises her arm and hollers, "I'm right here," and strides over. "What's up? I can tell, Anouchka, you've got something big on your mind."

"I do! What if we organize a clinic in France!?"

All she gets is raised eyebrows.

"Really. We could do it. I could organize it. I know how to do it. And my husband could help."

Frank chooses to be the voice of reason here. "I don't think that would work out too well."

Christine adds, "The legalities and fees of customs alone—"

Anouchka is not deterred. "I know it may seem crazy to think of it, but I want to do something. Something to help you, Frank, and the horses. But in my mind, how it works, it has to be something *big*. So we have a big impact. You know?"

Frank and Christine glance at each other. Both of them know the other's thoughts, crazy French girl.

Eventually, they get Anouchka to let it go. Focus on the now.

The clinic goes on, as a clinic always does.

Chapter 20
Horses on the Prairie

If you have knowledge, let others light their candles in it.
~ Margaret Fuller

2003 – 2006

"They're calling it *Horses on the Prairie: An Equine Science, Math, and Culture Camp*," Frank says from underneath his tractor.

Leo sits on a haybale polishing his pipe. "Oh? Who's paying for it and what's it got to do with me?"

His brother's tone strikes Frank a bit oddly, but he keeps wrenching on the tractor's belly and goes on to explain. "Sounds like it's funded by NASA and the American Indian Higher Education Consortium. It's going to be outdoor classes for both Native American children and non-native kids. Butch Thunderhawk told me about it. He's gonna teach something called *ethnobotany* and have kids do projects about natural prairie grasses and water and things like that. Thought I might want to be involved and contribute in some way. Maybe let the kids meet some Nokota. You know, interact with the horses, and learn about them.

He only hears a grunt, so Frank rolls out from under the tractor to see what Leo's deal is. "What do you think? Could be pretty neat. Workin' with the kids and all."

Leo doesn't make eye contact. "Yup. Neat. S'pose you're thinkin' it'll be good publicity too, huh."

Again, the tone seems off. It's unexpected. Frank thought Leo would be all over this. That's okay if not. He's just filling him in.

"Well, I think it would be great to teach the kids about the Nokota. They're the future, ya know. If we can help them get interested in the horses and show 'em how they're a part of their culture, and how they play a part in nature and art ..."

Leo hops down abruptly from his spot, grabs a wrench and some of Frank's other tools off the workbench, and starts walking off. "Yah, yah." He waves a hand. "Do what you want, Mr. Nokota." He gets in his truck and slams the door. Gravel spits out from the tires as he pulls out onto the road.

Shelly comes out of the house and meets Frank at the barn. "What was that all about?"

"I honestly don't really know. I told him about the *Horses on the Prairie* camp I'm going to help out with. He didn't seem real keen on it and just left. Took a bunch of tools and left."

Shelly looks down the road at Leo's disappearing truck. "Is it just me, or has he been more irritable than normal lately?"

"Oh, I don't know about that. Leo's Leo." He goes back to tinkering on the tractor. He needs to get back out in the field to finish cutting hay, but he'd hit a decent-sized rock earlier, and it got things out of whack.

Shelly stands next to the haybine sitting close by, waiting its turn to be fixed. "Yah, I suppose. I've just been getting an odd vibe from him lately. The way he comes and goes, right into the house even, whenever he wants, taking whatever he wants."

Frank's voice comes from the other side of the tractor, "Well if you look at it his way, if it weren't for him, we wouldn't have been able to save it. He owns this whole place now. I guess he figures he aims to treat it that way."

She hears the cranking of a ratchet and a bang, bang, bang after that. Her husband's words might sound fine with their living situation, but his actions look and sound like he's not.

"Call me crazy," Shelly says, purposely not mentioning what she's sensing, "but with his behavior and mood these days, and the way you two argue more and more, I'd say there might be something off with his meds."

Frank's head pops around the front of the tractor so he can see her. "You're not crazy, but don't go thinking like that." Wiping his hands with an oily rag, he comes around toward her. "Leo and I have always had our tussles. Been that way since we were kids. He's got a lot of troubles in his head from the war. I imagine his medications can't always fix those kinds of hurt. Not every day and all the time."

"You do too, hun. Your hurts may be different than his, but that doesn't mean you don't deal with them every day too."

"I know, I know." He pulls her into a hug against his greasy coveralls. "But I have you. And the girls."

Shelly sighs. "I guess you're right. We will always have each other." She pulls away to look him in the eye. "I just get the sense that something's brewing inside him. It's making me nervous. The girls are home alone when I'm working and you're making hay out in the fields."

"Now don't go thinking things like that." His leg starts wiggling and he looks around the place. He can hear music coming from one of the kids' rooms. Then he looks at Shelly and says in earnest, "I'll talk to him."

"Thank you." She smiles and swipes some grime off his chest. "Maybe it's time you and I think about finding our own place. Maybe someplace in town? Just to have our space, you know?"

Frank is not about to argue. It's not a bad idea. If that makes her happy, he'll go along. They're a team – in this together to the end.

* * *

Out in the fresh air on an open prairie pasture, a cluster of kids gather around Frank. He's going to lead them out to learn about and interact with some Nokota mares and foals.

Not far across the hill, he can hear Butch Thunderhawk teaching another group of students how to identify plants – which ones are edible, various uses, which ones can be made into medicine, and how to harvest them. He and Butch will switch groups after a while so all the kids can learn both lessons.

"Now, kids," Frank says, "let's stop here and just give the mamas and babies a minute to get used to the idea of us being in their space."

The children are wide-eyed and obedient. He motions for them to sit or kneel down in the tall grass with him. A seal-brown mare looks up at the class. Her spindly-legged black foal wobbles lazily under her. Unconcerned with the little audience, she keeps munching and blows out her nostrils. Then she nudges her baby to quit dozing off and get busy nursing.

"There," he points to her. "You see that mama? She's showing her baby what to do."

The children watch and smile as they see what Frank is showing them.

After a minute, Frank says, "These horses," he points to the other horses too, "they all have a social structure. I'm not just talking about the mamas and their babies. You know, the babies need all their elders to teach them the proper way to do things and get along in the herd. They've got their own language. Like that nudge she just gave him, she's telling him to get to drinking. It's lunchtime! Nap time's later."

The kids giggle a little.

He goes on. "The mamas watch the babies real close right away. This wobbly little guy here is pretty new. Only a day or two old. Just barely got his legs under him."

A collective "aww" and "so cute" come from the young onlookers.

"And then as they get a little older, the mama doesn't pay as much attention. She'll give him a little more freedom. That baby, the only way he's going to learn horse communication is to be a part of the horse society." He looks out a ways and points to a dun mare pinning her ears at a young horse who's romping wildly too close to her. "See that mare out there? That's the lead mare. She and a herd's stallion will dole out discipline to the young ones, maybe bite 'em or give a kick to help them learn how to be a horse, just like we have to learn how to walk and talk and learn our manners."

Frank's heart is full as he teaches these children about the horses. He knows they don't have much and don't get a whole lot of unique opportunities like this, particularly the youngsters from Standing Rock Reservation. He feels honored to give them this experience.

He shows them how to interact with the outgoing little foals looking for attention. Every time he hears a child say, "Oh he's so soft" or "I want to watch him run" or "Look, he's following me. I think he likes me!" it gives him hope. Hope for the Lakota horse culture, once so strong and undeniable. He smiles at how the Nokota could help nurture a reprise of horse culture – part of the promise he made so long ago.

* * *

"Frank!" Shelly says as she comes marching out of the house with her phone in her hand.

Oh boy, she looks mad.

He gets down off the tractor he was just about to drive out to the field with the hay rake. They've had a decent window of dry, sunny days, so he's anxious to get that hay up. Life for Frank this time of year is all about prepping for the winter months.

Shelly holds up her flip phone and says, "That was Christofer."

Her face tells Frank that it was not just a friendly visit. "Oh? What's he up to today?"

Christofer is a young, passionate man who has willingly taken on the arduous task of organizing all the documentation for the horses – what studs and mares are together and when.

"Nothing. That's the problem." She snaps her phone shut. "Leo won't let him on the property. Won't let him near it to do anything!" Her facial expression is completely perplexed.

Frank scowls in confusion. "What? 'Won't let him near it'?"

"That's what I said. Frank, how are we supposed to know which foals are from which studs if he doesn't let anyone out there? We know he won't do it himself."

He looks out at the field, then shakes his head and starts toward his truck. "I'll go see what the problem is. Get things smoothed over."

"Do you want me to go with you?"

"Nah, I'll work it out with him."

* * *

Frank will *not* be able to smooth things over with his brother. Instead, Leo will ban him from their parents' farm too. The reasoning will not be clear. It will not make sense to Frank. In fact, Frank and Leo will literally come to blows numerous times over the ordeal. One day, in the fray of a fight full of wrestling and rolling on the living room floor, punching, shoving, and swearing, Leo will break Frank's leg. It will stun the entire family. It will hurt Frank far deeper than the mere boundaries of physical injury. The real pain will cut deep, irreparably wounding his heart.

It will be a very dark time.

Frank and Shelly will buy a house in town and a small farm of their own just outside of Linton.

Time will heal Frank's physical wounds, and he and Leo will eventually find a way to co-exist for the horses' sake. The horses have bound them together in a way that surpasses sibling rivalry or ghosts of war. The Nokota horses will always be their common ground, no matter what.

The brothers' relationship, however, will never be the same.

Chapter 21
Cancer and Goodbye

Sometimes life hits you in the head with a brick...
Don't lose faith.
~ Steve Jobs

2005

Frank and Shelly's life twists down another, unexpected path.

"Come on in, Frank. Shelly." The doctor kindly ushers them into his office. He gestures for them to take a seat and he goes to sit down behind his desk.

Frank can't help feeling like he's watched this scene play out in one of those movies Shelly likes to watch on the Hallmark channel. He shifts a little uneasily in his seat and says too light-heartedly, "Uh oh. This can't be good."

Shelly sits perfectly straight and still, never taking her eyes off the doctor's face. "What is it?"

Frank pats her hand and gives her his everything-is-fine look, but deep down, he knows it is probably not.

The doctor takes a deep breath that sounds suspiciously like a sigh of sympathy. "Well, Frank. It's not good. All your test results show you have cancer. Prostate cancer."

Shelly's eyes go wide and her mouth opens, but she can't find words.

Frank works his jaw and starts to feel wiggly.

The doctor goes on. "I'm afraid it's not uncommon for veterans like yourself to develop it at this age due to extended exposure to Agent Orange in Vietnam."

"I know." Frank always knew that chemical would come back to haunt him somehow, just like his memories.

Checking the papers in front of him for an awkward amount of time, the doctor finally looks up and says, "I'd like to run a few more tests …"

Hearing the next word hanging in the air, Shelly finally finds her voice and says it for him. "But…"

The doctor looks up and, as though ripping off a bandage, says, "Based on the numbers and other results, I'd like to schedule you for surgery to have your prostate removed."

Frank and Shelly look at each other. Shelly asks, "When?"

"Today."

This time Frank's eyes bulge in surprise. "Today?"

"I think that would be best. Yes. Today."

"But—"

Shelly pipes in, "We need a minute to talk about this."

"Of course," says the doctor as he gets up and hands them a couple of pamphlets he'd selected already. "Go ahead and look through this literature. You can read about the risks and side effects. Then let me know if I can answer any questions. Just have the nurse get me. I won't go far."

Frank and Shelly both slowly take one of the pamphlets he's holding out in front of them. When he leaves, they look at each other briefly and then dive into the information.

Once they've gone through it all and discussed their options to the best of their ability, Frank knows what his decision will be. They have the doctor return. They are both filled with more questions, and the doctor answers all of them with direct answers.

Eventually, Frank takes Shelly's hand in his and says, "Nope."

The room is quiet.

The doctor asks, "Nope what? We've discussed a lot of options, Frank."

"No surgery." He looks at his wife and takes a deep, decision-making breath. "We don't want to have to deal with the side-effects."

"Okay, then." The doctor nods his head slowly. He gets it. Frank's wife is still young. "We'll go with watchful waiting then. That means we're going to monitor your PSA levels regularly. PSA is that 'prostate-specific antigen' I talked about. We can talk more about what your levels should look like at your age, but if those numbers get too high, we're going to have to do something. There's radiation, which is what we would try first. But at some point, we can also talk about the hormone therapy that treats tumors."

Shelly gives the doctor almost a pleading look. "Absolutely. We'll stay on top of it and make choices when we have to."

So they watch and watch until his PSA numbers climb to 100. Normal being 0-4. That is when they agree to radiation treatment. For nine months, Frank drives to the Bismark Cancer Center every day for a five-minute treatment. It makes him tired, so very tired. Plus, it carves time from his day – time he needs to give to the horses, make hay, and fix equipment. With everything going on with clinics, expos, and Conservancy business, it is an inconvenience, to say the least, but what choice does he have?

This is life. Now he deals with it. Can't get worse.

But it does.

* * *

On March 19, 2005, Frank's father Leo passes away at the age of 85.

Frank's mother, brothers, sisters, and relatives wait outside the Kuntz family home as the neighbor's team of horses wait patiently. Reverently, the driver urges the team forward. Their buggy carries precious cargo – father, husband, uncle, friend.

As the wagon starts carrying his casket down the road, they hear the sound of shuffling feet through the prairie grass. The rhythm of hoof beats drum the earth. One by one, the Nokota horses come to pay tribute to the man who opened his heart and this place they call home. Blue roans, red roans, dun, overo, black, and white – the horses nicker and whinny softly as the wagon wheels crunch the dirt, a procession of their own.

The team and buggy continue down the road, and the Nokota follow, quickening their pace and flinging their heads. Wildly entangled manes sail like wind-knotted flags. Tails stream a wake of prairie wind behind them. Hoofbeats pound harder. The horses follow the fence line, faster and faster, as far as they can go, bearing this man's shell with their spirit toward his final resting place.

It is a beautiful, undeniable scene of gratitude and honor.

Once the human procession gathers at the cemetery and Frank's father is lowered into the ground, they pass a shovel around. Frank takes the shovel when it gets to him, he fills it with dirt, but just before he lets the dirt fall, he stops short and looks at the black clumps on the spade. In a moment, he will toss this dirt on top of his father's casket where it will stay forever. Childhood memories flood his mind.

He is overwhelmed with visions of times gone by. Of working hard every day in the hot sun or the numbing cold. Of learning from his dad what to do, and what not to do. Of good times filled with smiles and fun, then some bad times filled with anger and regret. His dad wasn't perfect. No one is. He made some mistakes. Not everyone understood him or could tolerate his moods, but to Frank, he was a very good father.

That is how he will remember him. Frank decides that every clump of dirt on his shovel represents the bad memories. They go into the ground, and that is where they will stay.

Two years later, as often happens with those whose heart has been broken by the loss of their true love, Pauline Kuntz follows her husband. The hollowness of losing his mother, a saint among men, sits deep in Frank's heart. He will miss her beautiful smile and gentle ways more than he will ever let anyone know. Knowing she and his father are together consoles him, though. They deserve an eternity of peace walking side by side in heaven as they did in life.

A new era begins.

The homestead goes to Leo, the eldest son. At this point, the family starts suggesting Frank and Leo let go of this profitless life of horses and endless hard work. They should get rid of the horses and sell the land. Frank and Leo are the only ones emotionally and monetarily invested. Truth be told, both the brothers have seriously considered it, many times. Many a dark, cold, and rainy night, or blinding white, bone-chilling winter, both Frank and Leo have seriously considered letting it all go.

Frank has often wondered what it would feel like to have money in his bank account, take a vacation, or sleep without worry. The Conservancy would be glad to take it all on. They have plenty of rented property that can take on his and Leo's horses. The board wouldn't have to deal with the brothers fighting over who knows what all the time or disagreeing with their ideas of how to manage the herd, the breeding program, and promotional tactics. It would make life *easier* for everyone involved. It would make sense to sell the horses and sell the family land.

The thing is, Frank and Leo are Kuntz men, and that means they are stubborn. It also means they do what they know in their heart is right regardless of ease and comfort. Besides, Frank knows his own reality is that he needs the horses as much as they need him. He believes it's the same for Leo too.

This is Frank's life. His purpose is to fulfill his promise to them, and Frank Kuntz doesn't go back on his promises.

Leo keeps the homestead.

The horses stay.

Chapter 22
Competition

Alone we can do so little; together we can do so much.
~ Helen Keller

2007-2009

"We got competition," says Leo as he marches over to where Frank is filling the tractor with fuel.

"Oh?" Frank says. He knew this was coming.

"The guys in Minnesota. The ones that crashed that chopper, you know?"

Frank knows only too well exactly who Leo is talking about. He remembers the round-up when these people flew their helicopter recklessly close to the ground and tried hanging their leg down to shoo horses into a gate. They'd tipped the chopper just enough that the skid hit the top wire. The big blade hit the ground and a huge chunk flew into one of the pens. It'd been a big thing. News media even came out. It burns Frank's inside to think of how they'd denied their hotdog flying when he'd told what he saw.

Leo goes on, "They been breeding Shire and Quarter Horse crosses and selling them as *100% foundation Nokota*." He takes a huffy breath. "They can't use the name Nokota to represent horses that don't fit our breed standards."

Frank finishes up and searches for a rag in his back pocket to wipe his hands. He gives this a second's thought and then agrees, "If the breed standard is going to have any integrity, the name Nokota should have to go through our, I mean, the Nokota Horse Conservancy's registry."

"It should go through me." Leo gives a definitive nod. "I'm the one who came up with the name. I'm the originator!"

It's true. Frank isn't sure how these guys think they can just take on the Nokota name when they didn't have anything to do with its development. As he has learned time and time again, people with money tend to get whatever they want. That's just the way it is.

Leo is restless. His fidgeting and pacing, Frank knows, is a precursor to punching something.

"How about you set up a meeting with them? Take someone with you. See if you can talk some sense into them. You know, reason with them."

As though Leo hadn't heard a word Frank just said, he says, "I'm settin' up a meeting. We'll make nice-nice with them. Can even meet 'em halfway. We'll talk 'em out of it."

"Sounds like a good idea."

Frank knows how the meeting will go. His brother and whoever else goes with him will meet the Minnesota breeders in a little café on the highway. They'll all cordially shake hands and sit down to sip at steaming cups of black coffee. Tinny country music will play in the background along with dishes clanging and banging from the kitchen. Someone will mention something about the weather. Another will talk about a few new foals that show promise.

Frank knows the niceties will last only as long as Leo's emotions will allow, and at some point, they'll get to business. He can hear the conversation now.

"Listen, we appreciate what you're doing to support the Nokota breed. Minnesota seems to have a growing interest. And that's great. We understand that you've already set up a registry of your own. We're just asking that you not use the name Nokota if you're not going through us."

Someone will add, "It's important to keep the breed's standards and bloodlines aligned as close as possible," then gesture to his brother. "Leo, here, has the oldest, truest bloodlines. His horses are the closest to Sitting Bull's horses as anyone will ever find. The true native ponies of the plains."

Leo will probably get a little cocky. "I should know. My brother and I are the ones who picked 'em right out of the park."

One of the other breeders will finally ask point-blank, "Well, do you *own* the name Nokota? Have you trademarked it?"

The Conservancy had discussed this idea at several meetings, but when they learned it was going to cost over $2000 to do it, they decided as a board that they didn't have the funds to do it right then. They wouldn't be able to feed the horses. That $2000 would buy a lot of hay! The pursuit of a trademark was on hold, figuring there wasn't anyone else out there who would do it anyway.

Leo will answer the question. "No. We fully plan to, but we don't have the money right now. That's one reason we're here."

The conversation will likely go on and on, both parties nodding and telling their side, explaining their perspective and plans for the future. Once everyone has said what they have to say, they'll part ways with handshakes and sturdy nods.

When Leo returns from this epic meeting, he lets Frank know, "I think that went okay. We might've got through to them."

Frank is cautiously optimistic. He would feel more confident if one of the men said for certain and in plain English that they would not use the name Nokota. It chafes the back of his mind. Something is not sitting well.

"I hope so, Leo. I hope so."

Neither of the brothers feels like saying much more. It doesn't feel like a true win.

Not long after this meeting, they find out that the meeting had not, in any way, gone well.

While driving to Bismarck for his cancer treatment, Frank's phone rings. It's Leo. By the sound of his brother's voice, Frank can tell he is seeing red, "I can't believe they did it! The sons-a—"

"Whoa whoa whoa, what's going on?" Frank tries to calm his brother down.

"Somebody went behind our backs and got it anyway. Said right on the trademark application that, as far as they knew, no one else was using that name. They now *own* the federally trademarked name Nokota!"

"What?! How do you know that?" Traffic is getting thicker as he approaches the city.

"Castle. Turns out an attorney friend of hers just happened to be doing some research on the Nokota and looked it up on a hunch, and sure enough, somehow, the sneaky bast—"

Changing lanes to get around a semi, Frank lets the news sink in while Leo rants and cusses. This is what he'd worried might happen. Some people you just can't trust. Immediately, he starts thinking of what to do.

Leo turns on Frank. "I *told* you we should've spent the money. But noooo, you can't think beyond the next bale of hay. You went and talked the board into thinking like a miser like you. You got no sense of the future for these horses!"

Whoa. That is a low blow. It's the falsest statement anyone could ever make about Frank. He doesn't engage in Leo's angry comments. Instead, he says, "We need to tell the board about this. They're gonna freak out." He pulls into the clinic parking lot and finds the closest spot.

"They already know. And yes, they are freaking out. Blair and Charlie are on the hunt for someone to help us as we speak." Frank hears Leo take a few breaths then add, "I guess we got three years before it's permanent. In the world of federal trademarks, regardless of how you get it, if nobody contests it within three years, it's yours. Period."

"Then we have to contest it," says Frank.

"Yeah, no shi—" he hangs up.

Frank sits there for a second with the phone in his hand. They are going to have to take this to federal court. How in the maker's name are they going to afford *that*?

Here is where having faith in good people who want to do good things comes in mighty handy. As usual, it's the horses who call them to action.

* * *

An attorney from Atlanta, Georgia thumbs through a copy of *Cowboys and Indians* magazine while she sips her morning tea. She comes across an article about the Nokota Horse Conservancy. The article draws her in. She devours the words and rereads the story of the Nokota horses' struggle to survive and find their place in the world.

Ever since she was a little girl, she had wanted a horse. She looks at the picture of the Nokota horse in the article. It makes her smile to think how she had dreamt of waking up on Christmas morning and racing out of her room in her pajamas to find a bushy-haired pony waiting for her tied to the tree outside.

It was a silly childhood dream, the woman knows this, but something about the horse in the picture – with its soulful dark eyes peeking out from a frizzy forelock – speaks softly to her, beckoning her.

She reads of the Conservancy's plight and tells her husband about it. He is also a lawyer – a patent and intellectual property attorney for a major law firm in Atlanta. Somehow, they *just know* that this is their fight. They will fight for those who cannot fight for themselves because it's the right thing to do.

Over the next three years, this couple takes on this fight at great expense to their firm. In an amazing feat of pro-Bono legal gymnastics, they save the Nokota name and the rights to its usage!

They charge the Conservancy $0. The little ® will officially be stamped after the name Nokota henceforth.

In celebration, Frank and Shelly take a walk with the couple out to the mares' pasture near Sand Creek. Shelly has a picnic basket hanging from her arm, and Frank carries a blanket. They pick a spot on a hill that overlooks a group of mares. The breeze is light and playful. The birds soar through the cloudless blue sky. Maybe it's just him, but Frank thinks the air smells a little sweeter.

The couple has decided to become preservation breeders. They have asked to buy one of the best mares Frank has to offer.

To him, all of the horses are his *best ones*. Frank gestures out to the cluster of horses and says, "Take your pick."

The woman's eyes light up just like she is once again that little girl at Christmas. Her horse isn't waiting tied to a tree but grazing lazily on the prairie.

A beautiful gray mare with a long, flowing mane and tail raises her head and looks at the group of people sitting on the hill. No, the mare looks directly at the woman, and in that look comes a whisper. It floats on the breeze and skips from flower to flower. Then, when it reaches its destination, it says to her as if from a distant dream, *I know you.*

Then comes the moment both Frank and Shelly love so very much when helping someone find their horse. It's a magical moment, to say the least, something you can't describe with words. It has to be experienced.

The woman's eyes well up as she gazes at the mare. Then, slowly, she points to her. "That one there. She's a dream." Her voice catches in her throat, but she adds quietly, "She is *my* dream."

That is that.

Frank knows this mare is destined for great things. She happens to be from a small family in the herd that carries the dun factor which typically generates unique, primitive markings in offspring. This is indeed a special girl who will foal special colts and fillies for future generations. He is proud to send her to her new home.

Chapter 23
Thankful

Let us be grateful to people who make us happy, they are the charming gardeners who make our souls blossom.
~ Marcel Proust

2023

Winter is here. In North Dakota, that is always saying something. So far, the snow and the bitter cold are holding off. Christmas might not be as white as usual, but that's okay with Frank.

Frank sits in his little cabin calculating and crunching the numbers. Looking out the glass doors, frost speckles the hillside under the glow of the waning light. The days are short, but it's cozy in here. Surrounded by simple things and warm memories – plus knowing the ponies are fed, round, and fuzzy – he sips his brandy and listens to the playlist that Alecia made for him on his phone. Jason Castro's version of *Hallelujah* plays in the background.

All his horses are back in the dry lot. The rented pastures they grazed through the growing season need rest too. Even though it's not ideal, having them all close through the hard winter months is what's best for the horses. This way, Frank knows they're safe and being fed properly.

That means four round bales a day at $70 a bale, plus mineral licks. Feed for the hard keepers. Tractor parts and fuel. What good are round bales if you can't get them where they need to go? Frank is always doing the math.

Two more of his older mares have been taken into the comfort of a Kentucky farm. They will be so spoiled and so happy there. He remembers the tight embraces of gratitude he shared with their new people. He also recalls his last talk with the mares, alone in the pen that looked out over their new home and beautiful, green pasture. He made certain they knew he still loved them, would always love them, and how they would be so happy there. The thought of the old ones who have gone to their dream retirement homes makes his eyes well up. He's simply going to miss them.

He sniffs and bobs his head, taking a moment to think of the tremendous amount of things he has to be thankful for. He sips his brandy and reflects on all the great people who have done some great things for the horses before facing another winter.

A copy of *Cowboys and Indians* magazine lies on the table. He turns on an old lamp. His friend Mo Brings Plenty is featured on the cover. Frank's eyes crinkle with his smile as he flips to the article where the actor talks about the Nokota horses and his passion for their preservation. This man's sincere, genuine heart is evident in every way, especially regarding the Nokota. Frank thinks of all the help Mo has given. From posting a video with Roany, his own Nokota horse, encouraging people to help in what way they can to keep the breed around for future generations, to donating enough to buy practically two months' worth of hay. Mo and his wife are some of the most generous people Frank has ever had the pleasure of knowing and calling friends.

It makes him think of where he was some forty years ago and the immense progress he and his family have made. There had been times when he felt like he was the only one fighting for the horses, like only he and his family truly understood how unique and special this breed is. The memories become more and more vivid as the light outside dims.

Through the years, he and so many others have managed to get the Nokota breed into just about every major horse magazine in the country. From *Horse Illustrated* to *Western Horseman*, word about the Nokota is out there. They even have secured a spread in the book called *Storey's Illustrated Guide to 96 Horse Breeds of America*. Countless people have visited the horses for professional purposes, then left having gotten a deeper personal purpose. The little town of Linton has been the backdrop of newscasts, music videos, documentaries, movies, you name it, all in the name of promoting this rare and wonderful breed of horse. Once people are interested, the horses, as they always do, sell themselves.

Sitting here in his little cabin, with one sip left, Frank raises his glass in thanks to all who have been, and continue to be, a part of this journey with him. He says cheers for another year of continuing to work toward the end goal – that sanctuary where his herd can be everything their ancestors once were – to truly preserve the integrity of what it means to be a Nokota horse.

Just as he sets his empty glass in the sink, his phone rings. He sees Christa's face on the screen and figures she's checking in on him again. He probably should get going and head back to the house for supper.

He taps the green button, "Hello!"

"Dad!" Christa sounds excited, in a good way, not a worried way. "You will never guess who contacted me about a donation."

"The President of the United States."

Christa busts out a laugh. "No. Not quite. But just as important. Tractor Supply Co. in Bismark!"

"You don't say."

"I do say! Yep, salt licks and mineral blocks. Like a whole pallet full of them. Some of our friends have been a driving force behind it. We just have to go pick it up. Dad, this is *huge*."

Frank is having a hard time finding words. Again, people have come forth to help make sure the horses are fed and healthy through the winter.

"Dad? You there?"

His voice feels tight, but he answers, "I'm here, sweetheart. That's wonderful news. I'm on my way home."

Chapter 24
Loss

Do not pray for an easy life, pray for the strength to endure a difficult one.
~ Bruce Lee

2010-2020

Frank wrestles a stubborn fence post out in the stud pasture. By the way it wiggles, he can tell it is broken somewhere down in the dirt, but it doesn't want to budge. He gives it one last, frustrated shove and gets the post hole digger out of the truck parked close by and loaded with tools and a new post. He'll just put in a new one.

Being the Conservancy's herd manager is a job Frank is well-suited for. He gets to work with his hands, be with the horses every day, and make sure they are taken care of to his standards. The extra income is also extremely helpful when making ends meet. When he's not making hay or taking care of the horses at his own farm up the road, he comes here to check fences and fix gates.

Even though he's feeling a little tired today from his most recent monthly cancer treatment, he needs this physical distraction. With each jab into the dirt, he works out his frustration over the latest events.

Turns out, his brother Leo is trying to go off on his own. He's had it trying to work and play well with others. Not that Frank presumes he does any better at that task than his brother does, but Frank doesn't have an option. Leo does. Leo has the homestead. Leo has all the Kuntz land, so off he goes. Striking out on his own, becoming the Mr. Nokota himself.

Whatever. That's fine. Let him make his own website. Let him go start up his own registry regardless of the endless hours it's taken to create and maintain the Conservancy's existing one. Frank is just worried – Shelly and Christa too – that his leaving will tear the whole team apart. It might not. He supposes they'll be glad not to have to hear the two of them bickering anymore.

He stops to take a breather and get a drink of water from the truck. The view of the path he drove to get to this spot. It's on a steep incline and goes around some sketchy spots for his big truck. It makes him think maybe he should just use the ATV like Leo does.

In a lot of ways, Frank totally gets why Leo is going solo. He's a solo kind of guy, first of all, a lifelong bachelor. He's got no meaningful relationship, at least that Frank knows of anyway. He's charismatic in his simple-country-boy kind of way. People like to talk to him, and he's a great storyteller. He's already starred in his own documentary. *Nokota Heart*. That didn't turn out half bad. Frank and Shelly both raised an eyebrow at how they made him out to be this spiritual-like, mysterious, shaman kind of guy, but the filming did the horses and the prairie justice, really pretty.

Frank tries not to think of how it hurts that the film never once mentions Frank's name, much less his partnership and contributions in their journey thus far with the horses, but that's okay. This is Leo's time. He saved the Nokota and the Nokota will continue to save him. He needs this. He deserves it.

It's just that, well, it's just that this isn't how it was supposed to go. Not in Frank's mind anyway. He and Leo were supposed to be a team. Frank never wanted to be in the spotlight alone. Whenever he was interviewed, every single time, he made sure to say, "My brother Leo and I." In his mind, the bigger picture of saving these horses *always* had the two of them in it. Now that's changed.

It'll take some getting used to when comes time to show up together for an expo or a clinic. He figures he and Leo will keep their distance and do their own thing, no different than now. In the end, no matter what, it has to be about what's best for the horses.

Frank watches a couple of young studs romp and play bite-bite-kick. Testing their legs. Honing their fighting skills. They rise up, swivel on a dime, and send off warning kicks that *could* cause serious damage but never hit their mark square on. Then they prance around each other and fling their heads. Posturing like for a photo shoot.

The young studs are just like Frank and Leo when they were kids. Not a care in the world, they would fly around the fields and have horse-wrestling in the yard with all the neighbor kids. Never intending to really hurt each other.

Though he'll never let it show, Frank feels like this time – even more, maybe, than when Leo broke his leg – this time his brother's aim was true, and it hurts.

This is life. It's time to deal with it. There are fences that need fixing.

The years go on. Life does too. The *new normal* flows the best it can.

Then, everything changes, again.

* * *

On a hot summer's day in August of 2018, Frank gets a phone call that Leo has been in an accident. Leo had been out checking the herd on his ATV and crashed it. Something about going fast and loose gravel.

A few days later, on August 12, at Sanford Health in Bismarck, with his family surrounding him, Leo's injuries claim his life at the age of 69.

* * *

Frank sits alone on a big rock out in the pasture overlooking a small band of Leo's horses. It is a quiet morning. The prairie breeze does not feel like playing just yet. The birds have yet to sing their sunrise songs. With the sun's promise to rise lighting the east with an amber glow, Frank waits for it, but a small part of him wishes time could just stop for a little longer.

My brother is gone.

The words repeat in his mind, but they don't register like he knows they are supposed to. Leo is just on another unannounced trip to California or somewhere. He'll be back who knows when. He'll be back.

But he won't be. Not this time.

The band's young gray stallion, Frank can't help but notice that it looks so very much like Nokona did, way back (a lifetime ago) when they'd brought the stud home from that '86 auction. He's a snorty stud with a thick neck, legs like tree trunks, and a stubborn streak. He'll sire many great foals.

Brother Leo.

Two yearling colts play quietly in the growing morning light. A little bite-bite-kick will warm up their sleepy muscles and rouse the others. They might look like they are fighting, but Frank knows this brotherly roughness is just who they are. The fighting helps them learn and practice how to be great stallions like their sire one day. They need each other.

Leo is not coming back.

Frank suddenly finds it ironic that he has on occasion had visions of his own death, not Leo's. Never Leo's.

In the sky an eagle soars in a wide swooping circle.

Rubbing his hands across his weary face, Frank's mind starts wheeling. What will become of the herd? Leo had been letting it be for quite some time now like he wanted nature to take care of things. As far as Frank and Shelly can tell, since Leo branched off on his own, he didn't maintain a very complete registry. That's all well and good until someone tries to sell them, which they will have to do. There's just no two ways around that.

Oldest sister Patty tries so hard to help everyone figure out what to do, but it really is kind of a mess. No one in the family wants anything to do with the homestead. Even though it holds dear, sentimental memories, it's run down and needs more work than anyone, including Frank, can imagine putting into it. It will have to go to the highest bidder.

Frank will carefully select and purchase around sixty horses, he supposes once all things are said and done. Maybe there will be enough left of his inheritance to pay his debts for land rental.

An overo stud prances in a looping circle around a few mares and their young ones. Frank knows each of his horses by name. He knows their personalities, their temperaments, and their lineage. If he doesn't remember, there is always someone who does because of all the people who have been a part of the herd's life.

How is he going to figure out the sires and dams of Leo's horses, though? He shakes his head in frustration stitched with anger and sadness. It's going to be a big mess. After the land is sold, there's a very real possibility that much of Leo's herd will be scattered to the wind.

Two studs kick and buck and bite at each other with an intensity that seems to be more than just play. The smaller one lets fly a final kick that lands squarely on the overo's face, dangerously close to his eye. The overo's scream splits the air, wheels, and runs. This ends the fight.

Leo.

Frank will be asked to speak about and write tributes to his brother over the next few weeks. He will do it with an open heart, but the reality is, nothing he writes or says will do his emotions justice. That's okay.

He will scatter the bad memories with his brother's ashes to the wind when it is time. Only the good ones will remain, the memories filled with horses.

Meanwhile, Frank fully realizes all eyes will be on him to ensure the fight to preserve the Nokota breed continues, not just for Leo, but for all the people who have played a role, big and small.

* * *

Frank's Tribute to his brother Leo

This week we lost a man (and brother) who was very instrumental in saving a genetic phenotype and historically correct type of horse, the Nokota. It was his horse knowledge and expertise that helped save the Nokota horse.

It was a long, hard road for Leo, but at times very gratifying as well. Leo now is walking in lush green grass with abundant water and Nokotas all around him. He also has other family members there with him, brother Bob and sister Connie, and our parents, Leo, and Pauline. Our parents, family, and friends were integral to the Nokota breed's survival. Without ALL of them, the Nokotas would certainly not be here.

There are so many of you out there who have assisted in the Nokota cause. I know that Leo is so grateful to each and every one of you. You all have helped the Nokotas take steps forward, whether you feel you've made small or big steps, they had to be taken. So, I know he thanks you all for taking those steps. Because of everyone's collaborative efforts, there are Nokota breeders in both America and Europe. They are being used in all kinds of equine disciplines including fox hunting, eventing, trail riding, endurance, reining, cutting, therapy horses, etc. What was once a small Nokota herd of only 200 is now nearly 1,000 strong in the US and abroad. I know that Leo would feel good about how far these horses have come and where they are going.

On Leo's behalf, I would like to thank you all for your help and support, and I will continue to work to promote, preserve, educate, and help bring back the Nokota horse to the Native Plains people. These were all goals Leo had.

Sincerely,
Frank Kuntz, NHC Executive Director

* * *

A year later, while at another fall clinic in Pennsylvania at the Nokota Preserve, the floor falls out from under Frank's feet when he gets another phone call. This time, it's about Shelly.

A brain bleed says a voice on the other end.

Time warps around him as he tries to make sense of the words he hears.

Medevacked to Fargo.

This is not possible. Shelly is fine. Sure, she has some trouble with her knee, but the surgery she has scheduled in a few weeks – when he will be home for her – should take care of that.

You need to come home.

He is half a country away! The words coming from the person on the phone fade as the pounding of his heart migrates to his brain, muffling the rest of the world. His wife needs him. He has to get home.

As soon as his mind clears and he begins to think again, he calls Lindsay, Shelly's daughter who lives in Philadelphia. Lindsay, without a second thought, books a flight and swoops Frank up. In no time, they are on a flight to North Dakota – a flight Frank will hardly even remember – and together, they fly to Shelly's side.

Frank stands in the doorway to her room. Sarah, Shelly's other daughter, gets up stiffly and gives him a weary look. She pats him on the shoulder and signals him to take her spot.

"She needs you, Frank." The words linger in the stale, sterile air. Then she shuffles out to the hallway where the rest of the kids and some close friends wait.

The hospital room is dim and eerily silent as he pulls up a chair next to her bed. She is so still. It is so quiet.

Frank takes her hand in his and rocks ever-so-slightly. He looks up at her, fear and worry riddle his face.

"I can't do it, Shelly," he whispers. His throat is tight, and tears threaten to spill with each word. "I can't do life without you." He gently squeezes her hand and puts it to his lips.

It's true. He can't imagine life without her. She is the rock he leans against in the hardest times. She is his center and grounding point when he needs perspective. She is his cheerleader and forever teammate.

He looks up at her and says, "Remember that time you asked me if I ever had to choose between you or the horse, which would I choose? And I told you that wasn't a fair question?"

The monitor's hum is the only reply.

"It's not fair because I need you just as much as the horses need me. We make a circle – you, me, and the ponies. Can't break that."

He gets no reply except the blips on the heart monitor. Behind him, he hears someone entering the room slowly.

His daughter's familiar, soft voice says, "Dad? We're here." Christa, followed by Dawn and Alecia filter in. They stand silently by his side.

They stay like that in spirit for a long time. A very long time.

Eleven days go by. At times, Shelly seems fully aware of her surroundings and her visitors, but she will remember none of it, not one minute. Eventually, however, the danger passes, and Shelly is allowed to go home. Her knee replacement surgery is postponed for at least six months. In the spring, at her pre-op physical, the next wave of life's toughest punches hits.

Shelly has breast cancer.

She starts chemotherapy immediately, then goes on to radiation treatments for eight weeks. She will endure like a champion. Her daughters and so many others will support her like a fan club, and they will be in awe of her strength and grace.

She will win.

All the while, Frank is there for her. They take their daily chemo medication together, and they go in every six months for scans. Even in their battle with cancer, they are still a team. They do this life together, no matter what.

Chapter 25
Hope

May the stars carry your sadness away, may the flowers fill your heart with beauty, May hope forever wipe away your tears, and, above all, may silence make you strong.
~ Chief Dan George

2023

A bold and icy February wind seeps in through the cracks of the tractor's cab door. Frank cranks up the heat and keeps moving a bale out to the stud pen. The boys know the drill and quietly move out of the way without too much fuss. Even in tight quarters, the Nokota action looks more like floating than stomping or scrambling. Their bodies shift and sway around each other in a dance, the horse dance. Anticipation of a new bale always gets the horses excited, but Frank's boys know how to keep their heads about them as they wait for breakfast to be served.

He chuckles to himself as he remembers how he and his eleven brothers and sisters used to scrap over the food at their family meals.

He could feed the three or four rounds a day to his horses pretty much with his eyes closed, so his thoughts often ramble as he goes about his morning chores. Today, he has more than usual on his mind. Today, the Kuntz Nokota Ranch will announce its latest, and possibly greatest, endeavor. He's nervous about it too. It is, after all, crazy and risky, but his heart tells him it is the right thing to do for the horses.

He rolls out the last bale and drives to the open gate where Logan waits to shut it behind him. Then he picks up another bale from the stack and drives across to the mares' pen. Johnny-on-the-spot Justice is already there waiting.

Scanning each mare carefully as he gets into position to roll out their dinner, he searches for his hard keeper dun. Seeing her round, fuzzy belly makes him feel good, like maybe, just maybe, he's doing something right.

As he drives the tractor out and parks it by the machine shed, so much goes through his mind. Somehow, within a year's time, he managed to navigate through what seemed to be an impossible situation. He learned how to make it work. That's what his father taught him to do. Even though he still hates having so little space for the horses, they are also still safe, fed, and together. They are survivors. They still believe his promise to them is true and alive within him.

Frank is about to embark on an adventure he hopes will be one of the best opportunities he can offer the horses, short of their own sanctuary. He scopes the pen for the select mares he plans to involve. There's Tiger Lily's bald face peering at him through the crowd. Rayn nudges in close by, blending in with the others. Nightmouse follows. Frank stops. It's a little hard to believe – then again, the Nokota have a magical way of knowing more than you think they should – but all of them are huddled close to each other.

The scene is enough to make Frank's eyes glisten.

Sybil. Rugged Hawk. Rayn. Nightmouse. Cynara. Valentine. Sable. Starlight. Their blue roan, bay roan, and jet black bodies nestle around Tiger Lily's dun overo stark white face. It's as though they know they are in for something big, and they find comfort in each other knowing they've been selected for whatever important job Frank has deemed them necessary to fulfill. Frank doesn't want them to go, but he is certain these three-year-olds will be superb ambassadors of the Nokota breed as they become a part of this project.

Over in the yearling pen, he catches sight of Z Painted Warrior. That is one stunning black overo colt with bloodlines to boot. Frank's heart sinks, but at the same time soars, knowing Z will be leaving too.

Climbing down from the tractor, Frank heads with Logan to the warmth of the little cabin out back. He pours a cup of coffee for himself and lights a cigarette.

He snaps his cheaters onto his nose and swipes his phone to see the announcement that Christa has prepared. All he has to do is hit "Post."

It reads: "We are beyond excited to announce that 7 horses will be a part of the *Nokota Challenge!* We will start the journey to Texas in March where we will meet the trainers who will all be traveling from France!

Then the careful adventure will begin. They will be expertly handled and cared for as they make their trip across the water. Then come June *we* will also be escorted to France to see the beautiful connection between the Nokotas and humans!

The horses will be part of continuing the already established herd there. Check out their page and come along on this exciting journey with us!"

Frank involuntarily gulps. He is sending some of his finest horses to France. As in *across the pond*. In a *plane*. EquiFlight it's called. All to be a part of an event that has been named the *Nokota Challenge*. An event designed specifically for his Nokota horses with *only* their best interest in mind. Something he has imagined for decades. It's pretty hard to believe, but in just a few days, he'll take the select few from his herd down to Texas for the preliminaries. If all goes according to plan – and in Frank's mind, this is a gigantic *if* – the horses will be loaded onto an airplane and whisked off to France for the event of a lifetime.

* * *

The whole crazy idea started last fall at Christine Carapico-McGowan's clinic out in Pennsylvania at her Nokota Preserve. He remembers it like it was yesterday when Anouchka Khazizov insisted on a Nokota clinic in France. "Something *big*," she had said over and over in her delicate French accent, but he didn't think much of it. It was too lofty an idea with too many details and too much red tape. He'd been skeptical from the start. To be honest, Frank let the idea drift away as easily as dandelion tufts in the wind.

As fate would have it, though, Anouchka did *not* let it go. In fact, the young, ambitious, stay-at-home mom latched onto her idea and fought through confusion, roadblocks, and doubt. She was a French woman on a mission! A mission to bring her darling StarLight home to France for her four-year-old daughter, help Frank through his dire situation and bring awareness of the Nokota to as many people of influence and connection as she could.

Let there be no mistake, it was not an easy decision for Frank. He'd had nightmare experiences before shipping horses overseas. The required quarantine time alone for animals traveling overseas can be dangerous, much less safely getting the horses onto an airplane. His trust in the basic goodness of people wavered every time someone brought up the idea.

But my God, this lady was persistent.

If she hadn't worked over Christa's ear as much as she had, Frank may never have gone for it.

Thank the Maker she did.

It was Christa who actually called Anouchka to tell her how worried Frank was about being a part of the whole ordeal.

"Anouchka might be the perfect person to make this event happen, Dad," Christa had said. "She's a full-time mom right now, but her expertise is in marketing and events. Did you know she worked for a winery and did a ton of this kind of thing? It's her world. Plus, she kept saying how she really wants to help you and the horses. Yeah, she wants to bring her Starlight home, but she made it very clear that both she and her husband figured it costs too much to bring just one horse to France, so they want to bring a group over to make it more cost-effective. They're smart like that, Dad.

I think you might want to think a little more about this one. Anouchka honestly seems to have it pretty much all worked out, believe it or not. She just gave me her entire business plan and more. I think she's legit."

Frank ran the details through his mind.

"Plus," Christa went on, "even though her husband is pushing her to wait a year, she doesn't want to wait. She wants to do it soon so the event can benefit the horses *now*. She'll put up her own money to start the Nokota Challenge Association non-profit organization. She's already reaching out to some big-name trainers. I guess she's found one who was trying to plan his own event but had no horses. It's like it's all meant to be. Then she found more trainers who turned out to be super excited to start the Nokota adventure she's pitching. Her passion must have been catching because they all volunteered to buy their own tickets to fly to Texas for the *first touch*.

Frank liked the sound of that.

"You know," she said, slowing down with thought, "this woman has gone to her own strengths to help someone else. That's what we do. We find our strengths and we match them up with others, and somehow, we help each other through our struggles. That's how you raised us girls to be."

The pride he felt in his daughter right then filled him up. Her passion and intelligence and depth of heart never ceases to amaze him. If she believed in this impossible adventure, so would he.

* * *

So now, in a few days, he will take his select horses to Texas for their first touch with the people of this journey. Though he's still nervous – he'll always be nervous, that's just how he's wired – Christa was right. Anouchka might just be able to pull this off.

He taps the "post" button and lights another cigarette.

* * *

The twenty-hour road trip to Texas goes slick as a whistle. Traveling as the Fabulous Four (his nephew Brandon, Christa, and his grandson Beckett), getting there really is half the fun. They keep each other in good company, tell stories and jokes, and mess with each other while they try to take naps.

In no time at all, Frank finds himself backing the trailer up to a pristine, covered arena in the wide-open stretches of a pretty impressive facility, One Oak Ranch. Frank has often thought Texas isn't really that different from North Dakota in some ways. Maybe that's why he keeps coming back.

All sorts of people are already there with phones ready to record. The excitement and buzz is catching. When he opens the trailer door, and the mares and Z look out with wide, curious eyes, a hush falls over the arena. Taking their time to evaluate the situation, as usual, the horses stay for just a minute. The people observing hold their breath. Frank knows the people are wondering how these *wild*, untouched horses will take to the new place filled with strange smells and gawking people.

Frank knows exactly how they will take it.

He lets the horses speak for themselves, first one, then the next. Silently and oh-so-softly they float out of the trailer and drift on spongy, feathered legs into the space prepared for them. They look to each corner and sniff the ground, then they nestle close together.

Frank notices the mares looking for him. He steps forward just enough for them to make solid eye contact. Their gaze doesn't waver. He takes a few more steps toward them, his family. He doesn't know if anyone is watching him, and he doesn't care. The ponies are wondering where they are going. Will they ever see home again? What will become of them? The horses are looking to him for assurance, so he goes to them.

In his mind, he silences the commotion and chatter. He just wants the horses to know he is here. He won't let anything bad happen to them, not on his watch.

Somewhere from the corners of the past comes the echo of his promise. For one quiet moment, the corrals and people and buildings dissolve. The foreign land transforms into long, sloping prairie hills filled with songs of their ancestors. The meadowlark's plaintive tune carries on the wind as he perches on a sagebrush. Atop a coneflower, Cicadas trill and sway in the afternoon breeze. High above, an eagle's stark-white head glimmers in the sunshine as he soars in a wide, swooping circle, watching over the prairie.

Frank tells his horses, in the way only Frank can, that they carry their ancestors and the prairie inside them. No matter where they go, no matter who they are with, it is part of them, and that will never change. He gives these thoughts to them freely, with all his love. He promises them this.

Tiger Lily gives a comfortable sigh and begins licking and chewing. The others follow. Then, as though that was all they needed to hear, they reach out their noses and prick their ears forward showing their curiosity for all the people leaning up against the rails.

Frank eyes the people carefully, but not in a judgy way. He's just nervous. It's so hard to trust people these days, but he knows that the trainers have spent their hard-earned money to be here today, even though it wasn't necessary. He knows these young men and women must have the right idea to understand the importance of that first touch. Each will be paired with a horse and, over the next three months, they will create a trusting partnership and learn together. Then, at the finale, horses and trainers will show what they have accomplished. Three *months*. Not a long weekend. Not a timed contest at an expo. They will have three months to create their horse-human bond and learn how to truly communicate with each other. They will work at whatever pace the horses require, and they will get as far as feels natural.

Some may think that's not very impressive, but to Frank, it is a dream. These horses, every single one of them, from his own saddle horse Auto to wild and rough Target, all they have ever asked is that they are treated with honor, respect, and friendship. Frank knows that takes time.

When he looks at these trainers, they seem so young. That's good. Maybe they're not set in their ways yet. If they want to *continue* to work with this unique breed, they can't ever get set in their ways.

Over the next ten days, Frank will do everything he can to help these young people see the Nokota for what they really are. At times, the Nokota can be strong-willed and fiery, but at the same time, they will be kind and empathetic with an openness to friendship if treated with respect. Frank will show the trainers the horse dance with his simple sorting stick. He will tell of their history, tragic and inspiring.

He hopes – oh how he hopes – they listen.

"Frank!" hollers a cameraman walking toward him. "Lemme get a few shots of you with the horses and," he looks around and at a cluster of people around Christa, "and your lovely daughter! Can we do that?"

It's the camera guy who is here to film the event and get shots of everyone wearing the sponsor's boots.

Ugh, the camera. Frank isn't a fan. He's spent more than a fair share in front of a camera in his days, but it's for the horses – it's always for the horses – so he will cooperate.

Then he sees out of the corner of his eye that a couple of people are struggling to sort a few mares. That takes priority, so he springs into action and steps inside the pen where they're trying to scoot Z Painted

Warrior, just a yearling, away from the mares and into his own space. There's a lot of energy, high heads, and quick-stepping going on but to no avail.

Frank knows exactly what to do. With an easy gesture, he asks a couple of extra people to step off to the side. He looks to the yearling stud, puts his hands in his pockets, and turns his wiry body slightly to the side. His breath comes smooth and easy. The young stud responds almost immediately by stopping and standing square.

Frank tips his head, looks the yearling in the eye, and steps forward a couple of steps as though he is going for a stroll. Z moves off a few steps in the direction of the pen. Z makes a move to the right like he's going to charge past Frank, but Frank sidesteps light as air with just a single step to block the path. Z tries for the other side, but Frank is lithe and limber as he sidesteps the other way to block again. Then, Frank looks down, hands in his pockets, and the yearling stands still.

In a nonchalant move, Frank motions for two of the trainers to step in and stand on either side as a non-threatening barrier. Z Painted Warrior's ears twitch at the newcomers to this dance, but Frank catches his eye again and steps forward. The open corral is just a few feet away. A nimbleness charms his limbs like that of his twenty-year-old self. Using small, soft movements this way and that, eyes full of wisdom, Frank, and the pony sway in the *horse dance* to the echoes of a promise made long ago on a prairie breeze to a midnight stallion.

Nothing will hurt you. Not on my watch, Brother.

Without a single fuss, the young stud moves quietly into his prepared space.

As Frank leans up against the rails to watch the yearling find the water bucket, he hears murmurs from the crowd that has developed around him. Then he believes it is the cameraman talking to Christa who says, "That. Was. Magic."

Christa replies quietly, "Mmhm. I've seen him do the horse dance a thousand times, but it always gives me goosebumps. My dad has a gift."

The cameraman says, "Wow. It'd be so cool to film him in his element. Capture all those kinds of moments on camera, you know?"

Frank grins and shakes his head. It's odd how people think he's like some magician. He's just speaking the horses' language. That's all.

He hears Christa's voice brighten at the idea. "Are you kidding? That would be amazing!"

Frank already knows something will probably become of it. Another attempt at a documentary. It's a neat idea, to show what he does on a day-to-day basis to whoever might want to watch it. It sure isn't glamorous, but whatever. As always, he'd do it for the horses.

He can't think about that kind of thing right now. This preliminary time here in Texas is for the trainers and horses to get to know each other, pair them up, and prepare the horses for the flight.

The two trainers – a woman and a man, the ones who helped with the yearling – walk toward Frank. Their faces are filled with genuine joy. He immediately likes them.

They shake hands and exchange polite greetings. It's tough figuring out what they're saying through their heavy French accents, but Frank picks up most of it.

He asks, "So what's your plan? I assume you'll aim to halter 'em all. A little give-to-pressure. Leading? How do you plan to get them on the EquiFlight plane?"

The man replies, "Yes. But honestly, we want to do as little handling as absolutely possible because we want the horses to be ... em ... how do you say ... fresh? Like an almost untouched horse for the event in France. That would be most fair."

Frank nods. That's a good plan. He adds, "They'll need to learn how to trust you. You're going to be asking them to do some things that could be pretty scary. The long, narrow chutes they'll have to walk through to get on the plane? They're going to look to your training, you know."

Both the trainers bob their heads. The young lady says, "Yes, of course." Her eyes are bright with enthusiasm.

The man says, "Absolutely. We do that with all the horses we train. These will be no different."

Frank's eyebrows go up. Oh dear, they do have much to learn.

"Well," he says as he puts his hands in his pockets and looks at them earnestly, "I think you're going to find that it *is* different when you're working with a Nokota."

The two young people politely nod, but Frank knows that only experience with a Nokota will show them how true his statement is.

As the week goes on, one by one, under Frank's watchful eye, each horse chooses a person. Each pair has a unique and special "first touch" story, and Frank is honored to see the human/horse bonds unfold before his eyes.

Only doing what is necessary to guide their horse through the flight process – standing tied, managing reactions to scary things and tight spaces – eyes are opened and progress is made. Trust becomes palpable as the horses and humans communicate and learn from each other.

The human-to-human relationships blossom in the mix of it all. Stories are told, history is learned, and lasting friendships are formed. They laugh together at their mistakes. They hug each other when emotions overflow. They re-hash each day over good food and drink. The more the trainers work with the horses, the more they seek out Frank to ask him questions. They are visibly fascinated with him, and it becomes obvious that he touches their hearts with not only his story but his integrity.

All along, the camera rolls.

Over the days, Frank sees the horses shift in the beautiful way Nokota horses do when they decide their person – in this case, their trainer – is truly their friend and confidant. Tiger Lily no longer seeks his face out in the crowd, but Celia's instead. Sybel nickers softly when Pauline slides through the rails. Rugged Hawk nods her head, flopping her bushy forelock, when Ludovic scratches her shoulder in just the right spot. Rayn follows Billy around like a puppy. Cynara likes to rest her nose close to Maeve's arm when they take a break from learning. Valentine and Evan seem to have full conversations about who knows what. Sable enjoys it when Gillian tells her stories or sings her a song. Finally, Starlight's doe-eyes on Anouchka reaffirm their previously formed partnership.

On the last night, Christa leans against her dad as they walk together under the vast, star-filled Texas sky. She curls her arm through his, and they stop to look over the property.

"It's been a heck of a week, hasn't it?" she says, looking up at the stars.

"That it has," Frank says.

"Do you feel as good about this as I do?"

"The truth?" he asks.

Christa just gives him a *duh* look.

He smiles and breathes in the cool night air. "You know I have what some people think of as pretty unrealistic expectations when it comes to the horses. This time is no different. I'll never accept less than what is best for the ponies. You know that."

She leans back on one hip to give him a questioning look.

He looks right back at her and, in all seriousness, says, "I'm pretty damned amazed." A smile curls up under his mustache.

Christa's eyes twinkle.

He adds, "No egos. No ulterior motives. These trainers really are here for the horses."

"They're good people, Dad."

"They're going to do good things for the ponies."

"I'm imagining *great* things. Great people doing great things."

"Well then," he says and looks up at the sky, "I guess we're going to France in a few months to see how it all turns out."

Christa's eyes soften and she leans in to hug him. "I guess we are."

Frank chuckles, "Shelly better start packing."

* * *

June 29, 2023
Three months later. France.

The first day of The Nokota Challenge finale event has arrived! The seats are filled with nearly 400 people. The people have come to see this amazing, rare, and hyped-up breed of horse, the Nokota. They have followed it online. They have read all the local articles. Their curiosity is piqued to the max. The raffle tickets sell like hotcakes. Excitement is electric in the air.

Frank, Shelly, and Christa are escorted to a place of honor in the front. They know that this is going to be one hell of a show. Frank kept up on the whole team as the posts came through over the last few months. Oh my, was it amazing to see the progress being made! He is so proud of his new friends for doing what is best for the horses through the training process. Frank also appreciates the trainers' honesty. Not everything went perfectly. It was not all rainbows and puppy dogs. Frustrations and setbacks happen. How they are handled is what's important.

Mostly though, Frank is proud of the Nokota mares. They are, as he had hoped, excellent ambassadors for the breed. He is beyond happy that their bloodlines will help bolster the Nokota breeding program in France, not to mention the fact that it's a good idea to have his herd genetics represented on another continent. If anything ever happened to his herd in North Dakota, God forbid, he now knows the bloodlines he and his brother Leo spent a lifetime to carefully preserve will be intact over here in France.

Frank's herd is special. Frank's horses bear a history that none of the newer, smaller breeders will ever have. Preserving them, as always, is still Frank's ultimate goal. He will still work to find a sanctuary in North Dakota, but for now, he just wants to celebrate this new adventure.

Looking around the arena at all the people who have come to see him and support the horses, Frank is overwhelmed with emotion. He and the Nokota have been through so much. The hardship, the haters, the doubt, the disgrace. It has all tried to beat him down over the years. Like wind and rain eroding a mountain, his struggles have carved away at his faith in people.

This, however, *for this*, he has no words to describe the sense of generosity and care and commitment radiating throughout the crowd of complete strangers here. He looks around at all the faces. It is like nothing he has ever experienced. Here he is, in *France*. My, how the horses have taken him places, introduced him to good people and shown him amazing things. Their journey through this life together, though filled with strife and struggle, is one he will never regret. It is the Nokota who have shown him how to fight, how to forgive, how to live. He forces back the emotions threatening to seize him. It's all just too much.

Then, Shelly's soft and strong hand rests on top of his. He grips it tight. Together, they allow it all to flow through them. With misty eyes, he looks at his beautiful wife, and she looks back at him. She taps his black cowboy hat and gently brushes a little piece of hay off his new, red shirt. Always in his corner, she shoulders the weight of it all with him.

* * *

The event begins and will go on for two days.

It is beyond anything he ever expected. Each mare and their trainer take center stage in turn. One after the other, they showcase the unique skills and talents they acquired in their time together.

Frank grins from ear to ear the whole time.

Billy and Rayn dance delicately over poles and through other trail class-style obstacles. They canter in perfect rhythm around the arena as Billy proudly holds a red, flapping flag. The crowd woos and ohhs as Billy rides her right into a horse trailer. He even stands right on top of the saddle. The blue roan mare with the dark shaggy forelock, stands stock still with a sturdy stance as he climbs up. Her ears tap back to his every move, listening and sensing, making sure he is okay. The crowd cheers when he starts swinging a lasso overhead.

At one point, he brings Nightmouse out too, sidles her up right alongside Rayn, and hops onto her sleek, ebony bareback. This little mare gets a saddle eventually too. She is a dream to watch as she works her way through and around obstacles with the sure yet delicate footing of a Nokota.

When Gilliane and Sable take the floor, the scene takes on an artistic flair. Silken wings and liberty movements hold the audience captive. Sable's concentration and connection show in her carriage. Her eyes sparkle and her ears press forward for every subtle cue Gilliane gives. The little dark mare gives nothing less than her best as she shows she can dance and drive like a star.

Evan and Valentine take their turn, leaping over barrels, sidestepping like dance partners, and riding proudly with the red flag waving overhead. The sweet bay roan looks like she is having the time of her life, especially when her reward is a hug.

Tiger Lily and Celia capture the hearts of every person in the stands. The dynamic duo bond these two have created radiates from their very beings as they play together for the crowd. The way the little dun overo mare looks to Celia with those sweet eyes – one blue, the other dark – and nuzzles close to her when they rest translates one thing: *You are my friend, and I am yours.*

Celia smiles perpetually through their adorable, as well as impressive, routine. Sitting bareback, Celia shoots her bow and arrow. Tiger Lily doesn't flinch. When Celia straps a gigantic, cowboy hat-clad stuffed bear on Tiger Lily's back and they go flopping around the arena, they laugh along with the audience. Celia and Tiger Lily walk together, talk together, and steal hearts together.

Breathtaking Cynara brings an air of refined strength to the show. As Maeve shows, English style, how precisely and intricately this stunning and sturdy blue roan mare can move off of the subtlest cues in just a halter and lead rope. Their liberty work is inspiring to watch, as is the relationship they have together.

Pauline and Sybil are a fun pair to watch. Happiness emanates from both as they parade around with white netting and balloons. Hair flying – both horse and human – they joyfully show off all the hard work they have put in together in the last few months. Halterless, Sybil follows Pauline's every move. Sybil's trademark thick neck, blue roan coat, and tuned-in-to-her-human presence showcase her best Nokota features.

When Ludovic and Rugged Hawk enter the arena, the cautious red roan's eyes are locked hard on her partner. She shows how much she has learned from Ludovic. The noises, all the people, the energy in the air – it's all a lot to process. She keeps her ears and eyes on her trainer. The trust Ludovic has developed with her is a beautiful thing to watch. Anyone can see by the way she looks at him that Ruggy knows Ludovic will make sure everything is okay, so away they go playing with a giant bouncy ball, riding, and sidestep dancing. All the while, her ears are acutely tuned in – one toward Ludovic's calm and confident way, the other toward whatever element he asks her to face. They are partners.

By the end of the second sold-out day of the event, Frank is in complete awe at the expert hands that have partnered with his Nokota mares. Every moment has filled him up with renewed hope. That's a feeling he hasn't felt in a very, *very* long time. He's having a hard time recalling an event with the horses where he smiled so much, laughed so fully, or cried joyfully. What makes it all worthwhile is all the new families the mares are heading to once the event is done. The Nokota will go on to live their stories with carefully selected people. Some will be broodmares. Others will be part of therapy programs. *All* will be precious friends and cherished family members.

Frank stands along the sidelines as the trainers get ready for a finale of some kind, something to wrap up all the accomplishments brought forth over the last few months. They have planned something to punctuate how everyone is feeling – high on pride, excitement, and thankfulness. People are clapping and talking, all abuzz.

Frank is caught off guard by the tightness in his throat when he suddenly realizes he will likely never see these horses again. They will never see him again. It cuts him slightly, knowing he was not able to bring them back to the prairie where they could live like their ancestors once did. Their offspring will not either. It's almost like he has failed them. After they gave everything had – did their breed justice beyond imagination – for him. The heartbreaking pain of letting them go clouds the joy he has felt for the last two days. But he pushes such heavy thoughts down. They are to be dealt with at another time.

Then, out of the blue, the trainers ask him to join them in the arena. A little taken aback at first, he wonders what they expect from him. He's not really in the right frame of mind to give a speech of any length, but he goes with them.

Ludovic, Celia, and Evan have brought in Rugged Hawk, Tiger Lily, and Valentine equipped with simple long lines.

Ludovic says, "We want you to know how much we honor you, your story, your plight, and your love for this Nokota breed."

Frank just smiles and nods, not really knowing what to say. He has been honored to have been treated so well and accepted so fully here.

Evan adds, "And you know, Monsieur Frank, you were right."

Frank gives a cheeky grin and says, "Oh? About what?"

"About them being different."

Frank just crinkles his eyes at that.

Celia says, "Is true. It's not possible to explain, though. We had to find out for ourselves."

Frank places a proud hand on her shoulder, then Ludovic's and Evan's. He knew these kids would figure it out.

"Walk with us," says Celia with glistening eyes, and she holds out Tiger Lily's lines to him. "*Take the reins*, as you say, one last time. Please?"

Frank is frozen as he looks hard at the reins in her hands. Tiger Lily turns her head all the way to look him in the eye. Rugged Hawk turns too, and then Valentine. Like a whisper on a prairie breeze, they say, *Do this one last thing for us. Then you can let us go.*

All eyes are on Frank – the audience, the trainers, his family.

Slowly, focusing on the reins, Frank reaches out but doesn't take them. Celia gently places the reins in his hand and curls his fingers tightly around them. She meets his eyes and gives him a smile of such encouragement that he can't help but embrace this moment to the fullest.

Together they go.

The crowd erupts with applause. Ludovic waves his arms to get them even more pumped up, then he swipes Frank's hat off his head and waves that, making the crowd go nuts.

Something deep inside Frank's soul bubbles up to the surface and takes wing. He feels his chest puff up under his shirt. His body feels light and lithe as a child again. He finds himself laughing out loud along with everyone else. Tiger Lily flings her head happily at the sound.

The horses and trainers walk alongside Frank proudly, steps confident and sure. Everyone holds their head high. Their eyes are bright and their shoulders straight.

Then Frank realizes that everything about this whole experience has been preparing him – preparing him to let these ponies go live their stories, preparing him to keep up the good fight for the rest of his herd at home in North Dakota, and preparing him for new struggles ahead.

It has been preparing him for the future, whatever that may be.

Afterward

Frank and his family continue to work toward their goal of finding his herd a sanctuary. They seek a place where the horses can develop and maintain Nokota survival skills, rusticity, social structure, intellect, and unique language like nature intended. The Kuntz family dreams of a privately owned preserve with an interpretive center and horse therapy center. Their dream is to have a place where future generations can visit and learn about these amazing horses and their history.

If you want to learn more about Frank and the Nokota® and learn how you can contribute, go to kuntznokotaranch.org or like them on Facebook.

The End

Bibliography

Bell, Ryan T. "Sitting Bull's Lost Horses? The Nokota Horse Conservancy believes… by Ryan T. Bell." *Medium*, 20 August 2014, https://medium.com/@ryantbell/sitting-bulls-lost-horses-e2c9036d8284. Accessed 27 May 2024.

"C-123 Airplanes and Agent Orange Residue - Public Health." *VA Public Health*, 11 April 2023, https://www.publichealth.va.gov/exposures/agentorange/locations/residue-c123-aircraft/index.asp. Accessed 16 March 2024.

Carapico-McGowan, Christine. Personal interview. Conducted by Julie Christen. 7 September 2024.

"Frank and Grandsons." Doll, Nikki. Lil Redd's Photography. 2023.

Gandy, Jennifer. Personal interview. Conducted by Julie Christen. 7-9 February 2024.

Garland, Sean, director. *Nokota Heart*. Long Island Birdie and Yard Ireland, 2011, https://www.youtube.com/watch?v=VNI1LVsJxRM. Accessed 18 05 2024.

Hauge, Shelly. Personal interview. Conducted by Julie Christen. 23 June 2023 - October 2024.

Helm, Merry. Dakota Datebook Archive. "Black Fox." *Prairie Public Newsroom*, Prairie Public Newsroom, 1 May 2022, https://news.prairiepublic.org/show/dakota-datebook-archive/2022-05-01/black-fox. Accessed 2 7 2024.

"Horse Background and History - Theodore Roosevelt National Park (U.S." *National Park Service*, 3 August 2023, https://www.nps.gov/thro/learn/nature/horse-history.htm. Accessed 15 January 2024.

Johnson, Lyndon B. "Peace Without Conquest (1965), Lyndon B. Johnson." *W.W. Norton*, https://wwnorton.com/college/history/archive/reader/trial/directory/1959_1970/06_ch34_05.htm. Accessed 17 February 2024.

Khazizov, Anouchka. Personal interview. Conducted by Julie Christen. 4 August 2024.

Khan, Ejaz. "From War to Fighting Drug Addiction, Frank Kuntz | Vanishing Knowledge." *YouTube*, 18 October 2021, https://www.youtube.com/watch?v=FDeLNH0AW5U. Accessed 22 May 2024.

Kuntz, Frank. Personal interview. Conducted by Julie Christen. 23 June 2023 - October 2024.

Kuntz Nokota® Ranch, February 2023, https://www.kuntznokotaranch.com/. Accessed 25 July 2024.

Kuntz Nokota Ranch. *This is incredible!* Explanation of events regarding Frank Kuntz and horses. Facebook, 5 March 2023. Accessed 5 March 2023.

"Lakota, Oglala Sioux, Minquass Wisdom." *The Wild West*, 28 March 2020, https://thewildwest.org/lakotaoglalasiouxandminquasswisdom/. Accessed 9 July 2024.

Lyndon B. Johnson, "President Johnson Justifies U.S. Intervention in Vietnam," *SHEC: Resources for Teachers*, accessed February 17, 2024, https://shec.ashp.cuny.edu/items/show/1242.

McLaughlin, Castle. "Badlands Broomtails - The Cultural History of Wild Horses." *the State Historical Society of North Dakota*, 30 January 2023, https://www.history.nd.gov/publications/badlands-broomtails.pdf. Accessed 24 July 2024.

McLaughlin, Dr. Castle. Personal interview. Conducted by Julie Christen. "Memories of Frank, Leo." 2 July and 5 August 2024.

McLaughlin, Castle. "Nokota® History." *Nokota Horse Conservancy*, https://www.nokotahorse.org/nokotareg-history.html. Accessed 9 July 2024.

"Nokota® Blog." *Nokota Horse Conservancy*, 2018, https://www.nokotahorse.org/nokotareg-blog. Accessed 21 August 2024.

Nokota Horse Conservancy. "Frank Kuntz - Opening remarks, Annual NHC meeting 2021." *Youtube*, 16 August 2021, https://youtu.be/G0Npi2TFCyI?si=Lq8j0nncxbI0fwAq. Accessed 27 May 2024.

"Park History - Theodore Roosevelt National Park (U.S." *National Park Service*, 4 October 2019, https://www.nps.gov/thro/learn/historyculture/park-history.htm. Accessed 15 January 2024.

Ranchers.net. "Bad River Suicide Race at Fort Pierre, SD." *Rancher's.net Forum*, 14 April 2012, https://www.ranchers.net/threads/bad-river-suicide-race-at-fort-pierre-sd.57845/. Accessed 22 April 2024.

Ruppert, Christa. Personal interview. Conducted by Julie Christen. 25 June 2023 - October 2024.

Smith, Tim. "Sunflower forage and crop residues." *Feedipedia*, 2012-2022, https://www.feedipedia.org/node/143. Accessed 3 February 2024. Sunflower stalks.

The Dickinson Press. "North Dakota Nokota horse breeder dies unexpectedly, leaving herd of 200 in jeopardy." *The Dickinson Press*, 15 8 2018, https://www.thedickinsonpress.com/news. Accessed 20 8 2024.

"The Nokota® Timeline." *Nokota Horse Conservancy*, https://www.nokotahorse.org/the-nokotareg-timeline.html. Accessed 9 February 2024.

"The Story of the Great Plains ShelterBelt Project - A Brief American History Lesson — ShelterBelt Design." *ShelterBelt Design*, 1 July 2016, https://www.shelterbeltdesign.com/blog/anamericanhistorylessononshelterbelts. Accessed 15 January 2024.

"Uniforms & equipment from the Vietnam War." *Vietnam Gear*, http://www.vietnamgear.com/equipment.aspx. Accessed 19 February 2024.

"Use of Agent Orange in Vietnam | U.S. GAO." *Government Accountability Office*, https://www.gao.gov/products/ced-78-158. Accessed 16 March 2024.

West Central Tribune. "Nokota horse breeder dies unexpectedly, leaving herd of 200 horses in jeopardy." *WCTrib.com*, 16 August 2018, https://www.wctrib.com/business/nokota-horse-breeder-dies-unexpectedly-leaving-herd-of-200-horses-in-jeopardy?__vfz=medium%3Dsharebar. Accessed 27 May 2024.

Williams, Robert H. "Peta Nocona (unknown–1860)." *Texas State Historical Association*, 14 January 2021, https://www.tshaonline.org/handbook/entries/peta-nocona. Accessed 24 July 2024.

Julie Christen lives in rural central Minnesota. She has taught middle school for nearly 30 years. She and her superhuman husband ride a Harley and their horses whenever they aren't adding to or sprucing up their little hobby farm. They have two dogs, twenty named chickens, a barn cat, a fat donkey, and four horses, three of which are Nokota.